"A yo…
sented…
and ref…

It was going so well. She first served Billy, carefully pouring his coffee and then gracefully setting his plate of chocolate cake in front of him.

Then she got to Lee. Once she'd served his coffee and cake, she felt so proud of herself that she'd looked at him and smiled.

Her eyes met his. She smiled brighter. He, staring at her as if mesmerized, smiled back. And then. . .*it* happened.

She fell flat on her back!

She'd liked to think that there had been a reason for her to trip. But, in fact, it had been nothing but clumsiness. She'd been so overwhelmed that he'd smiled at her, that she'd stepped back. The heel of her shoe had gotten caught in the hem of her dress. And the next thing she knew, she was on the floor, staring at the ceiling.

She sat up and that was when she noticed everybody's reaction. Susannah gasped and came right over to her. Billy looked shock. The preacher stood up, looking concerned. Rachel put her hand over her own heart and asked if Patience was all right.

But it was the sheriff's reaction that really upset her.

He laughed.

KIMBERLEY COMEAUX has been married twelve years to Brian who is a music minister, a songwriter, and formally the lead singer for The Imperials. They have an eight-year-old son named Tyler. The family of Americans currently resides in Ontario, Canada. Kim turned her attention toward writing Christian fiction when she discovered songwriting wasn't for her, because she loves to read, especially romance. "I started out with an idea and before I knew it, I'd written a book length story."

Books by Kimberley Comeaux

HEARTSONG PRESENTS
HP296—One More Chance

Courtin' Patience

Kimberley Comeaux

Heartsong Presents

Dedication:

To James and Dianne Kennedy
My best friends who just happen to be
my parents. I love you.

And to my friend and critique partner
Debi Luna.
Thanks for all your help!

A note from the author:
I love to hear from my readers! You may correspond with me by writing:

Kimberley Comeaux
Author Relations
PO Box 719
Uhrichsville, OH 44683

ISBN 1-57748-636-6

COURTIN' PATIENCE

Cover illustration by Kay Salem.

PRINTED IN THE U.S.A.

one

Patience Primrose was on her way to becoming an old maid. At least, most folks in the small Texas town of Springton thought so. It was true that she didn't have many prospects, as far as potential husbands went. And now there were even less since the Reverend Caleb Stone had just married.

Patience sighed as she watched from her side of the room as Brother Caleb and Rachel Stone greeted the well-wishers attending their wedding reception. Patience had once entertained thoughts about the preacher. Every female in Springton had entertained the same thoughts. But Patience had been so sure that she could catch him. According to Emma Hadley's *A Young Lady's Guide to Courtship and Marriage,* she should have been the one walking down the aisle in a white dress.

She'd followed everything the book had suggested on getting a young man's attentions: batting her lashes at him, giggling when he said something funny, and always looking at him with adoration. Well, the batting-the-lashes thing was getting tiresome and making her eyes ache, the giggle was getting on *her* nerves, and she didn't always feel like looking at the guy as if he were the next best thing since chocolate cake. But the book had boasted that one hundred women had procured husbands by following Emma Hadley's advice. There had to be something to it!

Her mother said that she ought not read such nonsense, that the Bible would have all the information that she'd ever need.

Well, while it was true that she loved to read the Bible and prayed diligently to God, all she could think of was how the biblical Esther went to all the trouble to get her husband, entering a contest of beauty! She told her mother this, and Prudence Primrose was not amused, but then, nothing really amused her anyway.

So, here she was. Twenty-one and still unwed. If only she looked like the bride, Rachel. She had beautiful black hair and a lovely peaches-and-cream complexion. Patience knew that she, herself, was no beauty. Her skin was rather pale and her hair was a dull dark blond that she kept pulled back in a tight bun. She longed to wear her hair down like many of the other young women, but her mother told her that dwelling on hair and looks was nothing but vanity, and that was a sin. But even Emma Hadley's book encouraged "making the most of your God-given attributes and features."

Patience let her gaze slide past the groom and latch onto the handsome man standing by the preacher. Sheriff Leander Cutler was a fine-looking man. Tall and broad-shouldered, he stood a good two inches taller than the preacher. He kept his sandy blond hair cropped short, and his eyes were a strange golden color. Around town, the girls called him the golden man because he had a tan from all the time he spent outdoors.

Yes, he would make some woman an excellent husband. Could Patience be the one who could snare him? It didn't seem likely. She'd been trying to get his attention for a month now, and either he was dense or he was ignoring her. Emma Hadley's book said not to get discouraged, that patience and perseverance would bring rewards.

Well, so far it had only brought irritation from the sheriff. What was she doing wrong?

❧

Lee Cutler shifted from one foot to the other as he stood and tried to concentrate on what Caleb and Rachel were saying to him. He'd started feeling sick just this morning, and his stomach was now cramping so bad, he wasn't sure how much more he could stand. He wondered if he'd picked up a stomach virus.

Except no stomach virus had ever hurt like this.

The pain suddenly intensified, when Caleb nudged him with his elbow. "Lee!" Caleb whispered, getting his attention. "You didn't forget those train tickets, did you? The train leaves in a little over an hour."

Lee blinked and realized that Rachel and Caleb were looking at him curiously. *Tickets? Tickets!* Chagrined, he reddened, reached inside his coat, and withdrew them from his pocket. "Sorry, Preacher."

Caleb frowned and opened his mouth to say something, but Jessie, the little boy that Caleb and his new wife were going to adopt, pulled on his jacket. As always, his attention shifted immediately to them.

The room was looking sort of fuzzy, Lee thought. If he could only focus.

Why couldn't he focus?

❧

Patience looked at Lee with concern. She watched as the preacher and his new wife left his side and walked over to the door, apparently getting ready to leave.

She looked back at Lee and noticed that he was still standing there. Why wasn't he walking them out? Come to think of it, he didn't look like his usual vibrant self. Patience saw him start to sway. Frantically, she looked around, but no one seemed to notice him. They were all looking at Rachel and Caleb.

Patience did the first thing that she could think of—she scrambled over a row of chairs in front of her, then ran to where Lee stood, or rather, swayed. She reached him just as he began to fall. She threw her arms around him, all his weight leaning on her slim frame. She didn't know how long she could hold him.

"Help!" she whimpered, barely above a whisper. For a second, she couldn't breathe. She couldn't see, either. Her face was buried in his black vest, a button grinding into her cheek.

Abruptly, his body was lifted off of hers and blessed air filled her thirsty lungs.

"Patience Primrose! What are you doing with your arms around that man?" her mother screeched from overhead.

Patience opened her eyes and saw that her mother, Brother Caleb, Rachel, and mercantile proprietress Adelaide Hayes were standing around her.

"He was falling and I. . . ," Patience tried to explain.

"Land sakes, Patience. You ought to have more sense than to launch yourself over a pew like a hooligan and grab ahold of a man like that! Everybody in the church saw you." Prudence Primrose nagged as she helped Patience straighten her clothes.

But Patience wasn't paying attention to her mother. Her eyes were on Lee, who was conscious now but halfway lying in a chair. Doc Benson was bent over him, and Lee was shaking his head.

Patience shook off her mother's hold and knelt beside the handsome sheriff. He didn't look good. His eyes were clenched and he was gritting his teeth in pain. "How is he, Doc?" she asked fearfully.

"Foolish boy!" Doc said gruffly. He opened up his shirt and pointed to the tiny puncture marks all along his side and wrapping around his back. He ran his hand over the festered skin. "Looks like he got into a fight with a few porcupines. If they get infected, they can make you powerfully sick. It looks like he got into a whole nest of them."

Caleb nodded. "He told me about getting into them a couple of days ago. Said he'd been camping and accidentally rolled over on them. But why would they be making him sick now?"

"It takes days sometimes for an infection to settle in," Doc Benson explained.

Lee moaned and Doc snapped into action. Quickly he called a couple of men over to carry Lee to his office. Patience followed them and tugged on the doctor's shirt. "Doc, can I do anything to help?"

Doc looked beside him and measured her up quickly. "You sure can. Mary is gone to her sister's today and I don't have anyone to assist me. I'm going to have to clean and disinfect these oozing wounds. As far as his apparent stomach cramps are concerned, I'll just have to give him a dose of laudanum."

Patience hesitated for a second. Oozing? A wave of nausea bubbled up within her, but she quickly squelched it. She could do this. For Lee, she could do anything.

"Okay, Doc. Just show me what to do," she told him. Her voice didn't shake, did it?

Doc gave her a knowing look as though he could read her mind. But he accepted her help anyway. "Let's get this man to the clinic, then."

❧

It wasn't as bad as Patience thought it'd be, once she got past her horror of seeing all the "ooze," as Doc called it. Lee wasn't in any mortal danger, but he was very sick. The doctor said that he would probably run a high fever for a few days because of the infection.

After what seemed hours, Doc finally stepped back. "That's it, or at least all I can do for him right now. Let's just hope that we can get this under control. At least we got all the quills out of him." He walked to his basin and began washing his hands. Weariness was evident in the droop of his shoulders and the slowness of his movements. Patience had no idea how old the man was. With his dark brown hair that was peppered with gray and the crow's feet that fanned the corners of his eyes, she guessed that he was in his fifties. She'd known him all her life. He'd been the one to bring her into the world.

Patience finally got the nerve to ask the most important question. "Doc. . .is he going to be all right?"

Doc sighed and continued to dry his hands as he walked back over to her. "Yes, but he's going to feel a might poorly for a few days. And he's not going to be able to take care of himself. Unfortunately, I don't have the space to keep him here. And since that boy hasn't seen fit to find himself a wife, I'm going to have to find someone to care for him."

"I'll do it!" Patience blurted.

Surprised at her outburst, Doc just looked at her with raised eyebrows.

"I. . .I mean, he can stay at our house and my mother and I can take care of him," she stammered. Her mind was racing. What an opportunity! He'd be in her house, with her all day for several days! She'd show him what a good wife she'd make. By the end of his stay, he'd be begging her to marry him!

Doc nodded, his relief apparent. "That would be a great help. Of course, it will need to be okay with Prudence."

Ordinarily, she knew Prudence wouldn't agree to this idea at all. But, lately, her mother'd been acting so strange, since her abduction. Patience had a feeling that her mother wouldn't mind.

"Hey, Doc?" Brother Caleb called softly as he stuck his head through the office door. "How's he doing?"

Patience could tell that Caleb was very worried about his friend. *Poor man, he should be on his way to his honeymoon, not standing around outside of a doctor's office.*

The tall and broad-chested minister sauntered into the room. His black, longish hair had been tossed by the wind; the coldness of it had put color in his high cheekbones. Caleb Stone was unlike any preacher that Patience had ever known. Which was one of the reasons that she'd been drawn to him in the first place.

"He should be fine, Brother Caleb." Doc motioned for him to stand by the examination table. "He's going to be weak for several days, but, if God's willing, he should recover."

Caleb nodded but didn't look convinced. He reached over and put his hand on Lee's still fingers. He said a prayer over him, while Doc and Patience lowered their heads in agreement.

"Maybe Rachel and I should put our trip on hold. We can set him up in Jessie's room so he'd have someone to look after him," Caleb began, referring to his adopted son.

"You don't have to worry about that. The Primroses will be taking him in. Now, you just need to concentrate on taking that pretty little bride of yours and catching that train. We'll watch over him while you're gone. You just keep on praying for him, and he'll be fine."

Patience could tell Caleb was clearly torn. On one hand, he wanted to stay and be the one that looked after his friend. On the other, he had a wife now with whom he needed to spend some time alone.

"All right, Doc," he relented. He looked at Patience, and she couldn't help but cringe at what she knew he must be thinking—she was desperate for a husband, any husband. She'd been a pest around the preacher, always trying to get his attention, flirting. And now she was going to be taking care of his best friend.

Oh, he knew what she was about, all right. She'd made no secret of the fact that she liked the sheriff. But she prayed that he would also see that she was sincere about looking after him and seeing that he got well.

Couldn't they see that she was a good woman, that looks weren't everything? Couldn't they see that she would make a good wife, that she would love and cherish the man who would marry her?

Would she ever get the chance to prove it?

"Miss Patience, I'm much obliged that you're looking after him," he said finally.

Too tired to be coy, Patience merely nodded tiredly.

"You're welcome, Brother Caleb. I'll do my best to see that he pulls through."

Caleb nodded, and after one last look at Lee, he left the room.

Patience looked at Doc. "I'd better go tell my mother and then get the house ready. Do you think you can have him brought out before sunset?"

Doc agreed that he would, and Patience went out of the office. There was so much to do. The room needed to be dusted and the linens changed.

Everything had to be perfect!

two

For three days, Lee slept fitfully most of the time, burning with fever.

Patience and her mother were exhausted in their care for him. They took turns dribbling broth and water down his throat and mopping him down with cool water to keep the fever down.

Patience had really been surprised that her mother had agreed to Lee staying in their home. Prudence wasn't normally a kind person. She was usually the first one to pass out judgments and to tell someone what she thought their problem was, but she was not the one to help them. But three months ago, something had happened to Prudence, and she hadn't been the same since.

She'd been kidnapped by a band of outlaws.

Patience was not quite sure how it had all happened, because her mother refused to talk about it.

It all had to do with the fact that Caleb Stone, the minister who'd just married a few days ago, had a past as a gunslinger. The Jenkins gang had tried to kill him once, and when they found out that he was in Springton, they'd tried to get to him again. Only they'd decided to use the woman that he was in love with, Rachel Branigan, to do it.

They'd ridden up to the Primrose ranch and apparently forced Prudence into sending for Rachel. Rachel came and both Prudence and Rachel were tied up for hours while the gang made their plans of revenge on Caleb. Soon after, they were taken into town and they were released when the sheriff and his deputies had taken over the gang. Whatever happened to make her mother so different must have happened while she was tied up with Rachel.

Her mother had never approved of Rachel before that. She especially didn't approve of her as a pastor's wife, because Rachel had a child and was unmarried. It had been the result of a rape, but her mother and the rest of the town had called her an adulterer and had ostracized her.

But when the truth had been made known to everyone about Rachel's circumstances, Patience's mother had been one of the first ones to admit that she'd been wrong. Definitely out of character for her mother!

Although her mother was acting differently, it was a welcome difference.

"Patience," Prudence called, coming out of Lee's temporary bedroom. "He looks like he's coming around. I'm going to go make up some more broth. Why don't you go in there and check on him?"

Patience hopped up from the dining table, where she'd been resting, and ran to the bedroom. For the past three days, she'd been living for this moment, the moment when he'd wake up and thank her profusely for taking care of him and nursing him back to health. Maybe he'd see her in a different light. Maybe he'd realize that she was the woman that he needed in his life. Maybe. . .

"Where am I and what are *you* doing here?" he growled the moment she entered the room.

Patience's shoulders drooped. Maybe she'd just forget about the man.

Taking a deep breath, she straightened her shoulders and walked over to the bed. "Hello, Lee. You are at my house, and I am here because I live here," she recited calmly, folding her arms about her middle.

Sheepishly, Lee looked at the room, at himself, then back at Patience. He felt more than just a little petty for sounding so mean. It was just that he'd been dreaming about Patience. That was the whole problem. He didn't *want* to dream about the woman. But now that he understood that he'd been in her house and probably hearing her voice, well, it was a little more understandable. That had to be the reason!

The woman aggravated him. She'd been following him around for weeks and he was getting tired of it. His friends were even starting to tease him about it. Especially the preacher!

He and all the men in town thought that Patience, while a nice girl, was rather plain where looks were concerned. And she had an irritating way of giggling and batting her eyelashes that could get downright annoying!

And besides, he'd sort of decided to court the new schoolteacher in town, Susannah Butler.

"I'm sorry, Miss Patience. Waking up in a strange place made me jumpy." He tried to sit up and then winced.

Quickly Patience went to him and helped him to sit up by putting her arms around him. "Sheriff, please be careful! Your sores are still healing," she scolded like a mother hen.

Lee was so surprised at the pleasant way that she smelled that he didn't protest her fussing over him. She smelled like flowers. . .vanilla! That was it. She smelled like vanilla. He was about to take another sniff when he stopped himself.

Maybe that was what she wanted him to notice. First he'd be smelling her perfume, next she'd expect to go acourtin'! Well, it would take a little more than vanilla to get him to do *that!*

Carefully, he leaned back away from her. "That's fine, Miss Patience," he said politely, then breathed a sigh of relief when she let him go.

She straightened then and blushed, realizing that she'd just had her arms around him. Awkwardly, she smoothed her sweaty hands down her apron and looked about the room. "Uh. . .Mother is bringing you some broth. I'm sure you're hungry," she said lamely, trying to fill the uneasy silence of the room.

He fumbled with his covers as if he felt awkward and nodded. "What's wrong with me?" he finally asked, confused.

"Doc said that those porcupine needles made you sick; they got infected," she explained.

He was quiet for a minute, a puzzled expression on his face. "But I didn't feel sick after I got punctured with them. But they sure did hurt when I had to pull them out!"

"I don't know," Patience answered. "I think Doc said something about the infection not coming until days later, something about not being cleaned out after you removed the quills." She shrugged.

His stomach chose that moment to growl. "I feel like I've not eaten in days!" Lee said with a laugh.

"You *haven't* eaten in days!" Patience informed him. "Three days to be exact!"

Lee's brows shot up in disbelief. "Three days? Aw, man! I've got to get out of here and down to the office! I've got a hearing I've got to get ready for. And I promised Miss

Susannah that I'd escort her to the church social. . . ." He struggled to get out of the bed but wasn't having much luck.

"You missed it."

Lee's head snapped up and his brows lowered in a frown. "Huh?"

Patience looked at the man and wondered why she was even trying to get his attention. The man was so dense. And it hurt more than she thought it would to know that he was interested in the schoolteacher. "I said that you missed it. The church social was last night," she explained, with just a little hint of satisfaction.

He groaned but kept up the effort until he was sitting up in bed with his feet on the floor. "Oh, well. I still need to get to the office."

Patience walked around the bed and stood in front of him. She put her hands on her slim hips and glared at him. "You are not going to go anywhere! Billy Aaron has been running things and doing just fine. Nothing much ever happens, anyway. So you just get back in that bed and rest!" she ordered firmly.

For a moment, Lee could do nothing but stare at her. Mercy, she was a fussy package of goods! Never would he have believed that mousy, little Patience Primrose could be so bossy. And she hadn't batted her lashes once since she'd been talking to him. He didn't know whether to be irritated at her boldness or applaud her for being so gutsy.

Instead, he just gave in and fell back into the bed. Lord knew he was tired. And having to deal with this woman just made him more tired.

She smiled with obvious satisfaction. "Mama will bring

your broth shortly." She walked to the bed table and took the worn Bible from the drawer. "Why don't I read something to you while we wait?"

Lee eyed her warily and thought that there was something fishy about the gleam in her eyes. But it *was* the Bible—how deceptive could she be?

Without waiting for his answer, Patience pulled up a chair and opened up the Bible. "Okay, let's see. I'll just begin where I left off reading this morning." She glanced at Lee, then back to the page, and began, "Song of Solomon 4:3: 'Thy lips are like a thread of scarlet, and thy speech is comely: thy temples are like a piece of a pomegranate within thy locks. Thy neck is like the tower of David builded for an armoury, whereon. . .' "

"Stop!" Lee quickly interjected, seeing where the Scripture was heading. Patience looked at him, a question in her expression. "Uh. . .I think I'd just rather rest, if ya don't mind."

Patience smiled an innocent smile that Lee didn't believe for a minute! "Well, okay, Sheriff. If you're sure."

"I'm sure," he said quickly. Was it him, or was it getting warm in the room?

She shrugged as if fighting to keep back a grin. "I just find the Song of Solomon so romantic, don't you?" she asked sweetly.

"Uh. . .I guess so," he muttered uneasily, very uncomfortable with the subject.

He may be irritated with her, but at least she'd gotten his notice. It was quite an experience to have Leander Cutler's full attention. In chapter four of Miss Hadley's book, it stated, "To procure the young man's notice, you must first make certain that he knows who you are!

Engaging him in witty and clever conversations is vital in this delicate process."

Well, the sheriff may not be bowled over by her attempt at witty conversation, but he definitely knew she was alive!

At that moment, Prudence came into the room, carrying a wooden tray laden with a bowl of delicious-smelling broth.

Lee wasted no time in spooning the warm liquid into his mouth. He was so hungry, but he had a feeling that the broth wasn't going to fill the void. By the time he was through, his strength was drained and he was grateful when Prudence took the tray and both she and Patience left the room.

Carefully he scooted down to lie flat. He thoughtfully fingered the bandage at his waist. He really should have taken care of this when it'd happened. He knew that porcupine needles could make him sick if the wounds became infected; he just didn't realize how sick.

He was sorry, too, that it had made him miss that church social. He'd been interested in the new schoolteacher, Susannah Butler, ever since she'd arrived just two months ago. They'd spoken a few times at church and he'd finally gotten enough nerve to ask her to the social. He'd felt lucky that she'd agreed to go with him. He knew that, because she was so pretty, there'd been many eligible men who had shown her interest. Her hair was a glorious auburn that she kept knotted at her nape, while little curls fell all about her face. Her skin was pale and dusted with a coating of very light freckles that danced across her nose and cheekbones. When she looked at him with those blue-green eyes of hers, it could knock the breath right out of him! He'd figured that she would already have a date, but amazingly she said yes to him. Now he wondered if she'd gone with someone else.

He hoped not. He figured that it was getting time for him to marry and have a family. Miss Butler would make the perfect wife.

❧

Patience sat at the sturdy wooden table, absently running a finger along the wood grains.

She looked up when her mother sat down beside her. Prudence wore a worried expression, and Patience had a feeling that she wanted to talk to her. She felt suddenly confused—her mother dictated, but never communicated openly and certainly never worried.

"What's wrong, Mama?" Patience asked warily.

Prudence looked at her daughter strangely for a moment, as if she wanted to say something. Patience wished that she would. She wished that she could pour out her heart to her mother and then be given a comforting hug as she'd seen other mothers do with their daughters.

But, as usual, Prudence did none of those things. The moment passed and Prudence shook her head. "Nothing," she murmured, then turned toward the sink and began washing a pot.

Patience sighed. If she didn't talk about the feelings swirling around her, she'd just break down and never stop crying. Why was it so difficult for people to love her? Her mother didn't show that she loved her, she didn't have any friends who expressed such emotions, and the sheriff definitely didn't love her and didn't show any signs of starting!

Sometimes she even wondered if God loved her. It

seemed a selfish and silly thing to contemplate, but she found herself thinking it anyway. There were so many people who were smarter, more upstanding, and better looking than she was. Why would God bother with a plain, average country girl like herself?

Then again, she thought, why would anyone?

three

The next day, Lee felt a little more like himself and not nearly as tired as he had been the day before. His stomach still ached, but he was able to sit up on his own—thank God!—and needed no more help from Patience.

It wasn't that he was bothered yesterday when she'd helped him up. Why would that bother him? She was just an acquaintance. A distant acquaintance. One that just happened to help him out in his time of need. That was all.

And he would have really believed that, except for the dreams. . . .

For goodness' sake, he didn't even want to think about them! They were ridiculous! In his dreams, Patience was so different. Pretty, even. And he'd been holding her hand and kissing her tenderly. She stood in his house as if she belonged there. Ridiculous!

He really needed to concentrate on getting out of here and going home. That was the answer. And besides, he knew that she liked him, and he didn't want her getting any wrong ideas!

❧

The only "idea" that Patience was getting was that if she wanted to get the sheriff to start thinking of her as serious courting material, she was going to have to work harder!

Eagerly, she opened Emma Hadley's book and turned to chapter five.

Upon occasion one might encounter certain problems pertaining to the young man, himself. One problem might be if he has shown significant interest in another young woman. Miss Emma wants to assure you that, unless there has been an engagement announced, all hope is not lost!

Study the young woman who has captured his regard. Perhaps she wears her hair a certain way or carries herself in a manner that is attractive to him. One can garner much insight on studying one's rival. . . .

Thoughtfully, Patience bookmarked her page and closed the volume. *Studying one's rival. . .* Hmm. Maybe if she learned what he liked about Susannah Butler, she could become more of what he wanted.

Taking a fortified breath, she put the book down and started toward the sheriff's room. She had work to do.

When she entered the bedroom, she was surprised to see Lee sitting up. He looked up, scowled at her, then stood carefully.

Patience merely folded her arms around her middle and sighed. Then she waited. Sure enough, he stumbled, rocked unsteadily on his feet, then plopped back down on the bed.

She'd already watched him do this three times today!

He glanced her way again and growled, "Don't say it."

She put on an innocent face and raised her arms in a "surrender" position. "I didn't say a word."

He let out a long, weary breath and sank back down onto his pillows. "I've got things to do. I don't have time to be laid up like some invalid!"

Patience made a show of smoothing her brown cotton skirt, then took the seat next to the bed. "Well, I have something that I think might cheer you up," she said pleasantly. "I've asked Billy Aaron to stop by and fill you in on what's been happening at work. He'll be here in a few minutes."

Patience was rewarded with an unexpected smile. She found herself smiling back.

Lee watched the smile transform her ordinary face into something quite. . .pretty, actually. Her eyes sparkled and her cheeks bloomed with color.

Not that he noticed such things, of course. He was just touched that she would think of inviting Billy over so that he could catch up on what he'd missed. There were several cases that had been worrying him since he'd awakened the day before. And talking to Billy would certainly ease his mind.

He wondered if it would be impolite to ask about Miss Susannah. Taking another look at her face and how she was looking at him, he decided it would be. And it would probably hurt her feelings.

"Well," he said, breaking the moment, "I appreciate you asking Billy over."

She blushed at his acknowledgment and looked down at her hands. "I knew you were worried and. . ." She drifted off with a shrug.

He looked around the room and racked his brain trying to think of something to say. "Uh. . .would you like to stay and visit with us when he arrives?"

She looked at him quickly, and Lee saw a strange look pass over her features. "No!" she practically shouted, then took a deep breath. "I mean. . .no. I'm sure that you have outlaw and crime things to talk about and it would only be a hindrance having a female in the room. And besides, I have somewhere I need to be."

He raised his eyebrows, wondering at her reaction. "Oh? Where are you going?"

"Nowhere."

He scratched his head. "But you just said. . ."

"I meant," she interrupted, "that I have nowhere special to go. I've just got some things to do, is all. Is there anything else you want to ask me?" she demanded with exasperation.

Women! Who could figure them out? She was making his head hurt. "All right, all right! I was just making conversation!" he said defensively.

"Oh. Well. . ." She glanced at the clock on the wall, just beyond the tall bedpost. A knock sounded from the other room, and they could both hear Patience's mother opening the front door.

Patience hopped out of her chair. "Well, that will be Billy. Have a good visit." She hurried toward the bedroom door.

"Thanks. I will!" he called after her, but he wasn't sure she'd heard him. What was wrong with the woman? And where was she going that made her not want to tell him? Not that it was any of his business. It just seemed strange that she was so reluctant to tell him.

Then a thought hit him. What if she was meeting a man? Did Patience have a beau? He laughed under his breath at that thought. Of course not. It was clear as spring water that she was still interested in him. Meeting a man? Not likely!

But then again—

"Hey, Buddy! Did you decide to join the livin'?" Billy Aaron asked cheerfully as he let himself into the bedroom.

Lee greeted his friend and deputy, but his mind was only on half of the conversation.

One question kept buzzing around his mind.

What was Patience up to?

❧

Her mother would have said that she was up to no good! But that didn't stop Patience from knocking on the door of her rival for Lee's affection, Miss Susannah Butler.

The door opened and a very pretty, tall redhead appeared on the other side. Her dress was something out of those fashion magazines that Mrs. Hayes kept in her store. Made of light blue-green linen and trimmed in delicate lace, it fit her figure perfectly. The color even matched her eyes. Like most redheads, she had pale skin, and even her freckles added, rather than took away from her beauty.

She was everything that Patience wished that she could be—elegant, graceful, and beautiful.

Holding back a sigh, Patience held out the pecan pie that she had brought with her. "Hello, Miss Butler. I'm Patience Primrose. I've not made your acquaintance since you've arrived in town, so I thought I'd come by and welcome you to Springton," Patience recited with more enthusiasm than she felt.

Susannah's face lit up in a delighted smile. "Well, aren't you the sweetest little ol' thang!" she exclaimed in a soft Southern drawl that took Patience by surprise. "Is that delicious-smelling pie for me?"

Bemused, Patience simply nodded her head. Susannah

Butler was a Southern belle? Maybe that's the attraction. . . .

"Well, won't you come in? I've been so busy with the school that I haven't had time to meet many folks around here. Here let me take that," she said as she took the pie from Patience's hands and ushered her into the little house.

Visiting with Susannah was an eye-opening experience for Patience. Never had she met a woman who could talk as much as she! In fact, Patience couldn't remember saying more than fifteen words the whole thirty minutes that she visited.

And she learned more about her than she ever thought she would in just one visit. She learned that Susannah was from Charleston and that she was Bobby Joe Aaron's late wife's sister. But most importantly, she learned that although Susannah was acquainted with Lee, she didn't seem all *that* interested in him. Who she did seem more interested in and talked about in length was her brother-in-law, Bobby Joe.

Interesting.

Patience did come to some theories about what attracted Lee to Susannah, though. It was quite simple, actually.

He liked her Southern accent.

So she'd just have to. . .get one.

❧

After Billy left, finding himself all alone, Lee took the time to really talk to God and thank Him for sparing his life. According to Doc, he was lucky that he didn't get bit by one of those animals. If the creature had been infected with rabies, Lee might have even died from it.

That really shook him up. Up until now, he'd thought

of himself as pretty invincible. As a Texas Ranger and a lawman, he'd faced danger and life-threatening situations many times, but he'd never been affected as he was now. Suddenly he was looking over his life and was unsatisfied at what he saw. He knew since making a new commitment to Christ he'd taken a step in the right direction, but he still had some growing to do.

He realized what he wanted was a family. A home, wife, and kids, and maybe a dog or two. Maybe it was because his best friend, Preacher Caleb Stone, had just gotten himself hitched. Whatever it was, he knew that he wanted it more than ever.

The pretty face of Susannah Butler came to mind and he wondered if she was the one for him. She certainly seemed perfect. He could look at her and listen to her talk for hours. But was that enough on which to base a relationship? He knew also that she was a Christian, and that was the most important thing.

Quietly he bowed his head as he sat up in his bed and prayed. "Dear Lord, I pray that You show me the direction that You want me to go. If it's Your will that I marry, I pray that You bring the right woman into my life, like You did for the preacher. I also want to thank You for sparing my life and making me realize just how precious life is. I pray that I may be a man after Your own heart, Lord. Thank You. In Your name I pray. Amen."

What did God have in store for his life? He couldn't help but feel that whatever it was, it was going to happen soon. He didn't know why he thought this, but he just knew.

❧

Patience, standing just outside of Lee's bedroom door,

leaned silently against the doorframe and closed her eyes. *He was praying for God to send him a wife!*

What would it be like to be loved by a man like Lee? A man who took time to talk to God and thank Him for his life. Such a man would never ignore the ones that he loved and never would he allow them to feel neglected or unloved. His wife would feel cherished and secure.

She would just have to work harder. She must become someone that he would love. Someone like Susannah Butler.

Someone. . .other than plain old Patience.

four

"Good mornin', Sheriff," a singsong voice sounded through his sleep-fogged brain. For some reason, a vision of Susannah Butler arose in his mind. It was the voice that made him think of her. It sounded strangely. . . Southern.

He peeped out of one eye to see who was in his room and all he saw was Patience standing there. He knew it was just too good to be true to think that Susannah had come to pay him a visit. He sighed and opened the other eye. Patience was carrying a tray piled with a lot more food than they'd been feeding him before. His stomach growled with anticipation.

"Is that eggs and bacon I smell?" he asked, his voice heavy with sleep.

Patience smiled, batting her lashes. "Why, it sho' enough is!" she exclaimed in her newly practiced accent.

Lee looked at her as if she'd just spoken in a foreign language. "What's wrong with your voice?"

She placed the tray across his lap. "Whatever do you mean, Sheriff?" she drawled, giving him another smile and another round of extremely fast eye batting.

"You sound funny, and you're starting to do that thing again with your eyes," he told her bluntly as he picked up his fork and scooped up a good-sized helping of eggs.

Patience frowned and her shoulders drooped. If Susannah were here, he wouldn't say that she sounded funny! She made a quick mental note to never bat her eyes again. Emma Hadley couldn't be correct about everything!

She cleared her throat. "Uh. . .it must be the spring air. . .or. . .something," she explained lamely.

He didn't seem to hear her, though. He was much too busy eating.

Ignored again, she thought. She looked about the room, then down at her wringing hands. "Well, I'll just leave you to your breakfast," she muttered and started out of the room.

Patience stopped, not quite believing that she had heard him correctly. Slowly, she turned toward him. Against her better judgment, hope started to bloom within her chest.

Lee motioned toward the chair by the bed. "Why don't you keep me company? Unless. . .you have something to do?" he asked sincerely.

The cows had to be milked, the eggs needed to be gathered, and the chickens needed to be fed. "No," she heard herself answer. "I can stay for a few minutes."

Lee saw the hopeful expression on Patience's face and had a moment of doubt. He didn't want her to think that he was attracted to her, but he found himself enjoying her company. For the last two days, he'd found Patience to be surprisingly easy to talk to. She was intelligent and funny, at least when she wasn't trying to spin her feminine wiles on him.

He hoped that she would realize that they could be friends and get over her apparent infatuation!

He took another bite of his food and swallowed. "I was just wondering if you can fill me in on what's been happening around here in the last few days? Billy let me know about what's been going on as far as the law goes, but I feel like the world kept spinning and living and I slept right through it."

Patience put on a saucy grin and sat in the chair beside him. "You're not telling me that you want to know all the gossip in town, are you?"

He took on a look of mock indignation. "Hasn't anyone ever told you that men don't gossip?" he admonished.

Patience scoffed at that statement. "Someone forgot to tell Mr. Harold Ray about that. If it's worth knowing, he probably knows about it. Of course, he probably hears it from Miz Hayes," she told him, speaking of the storekeeper and her beau.

"You have a point," he agreed, smiling.

For a moment they sat in silence as he finished the rest of his breakfast. He wiped his mouth with his napkin, and Patience took the tray and placed it on the bedside table.

"Now," Lee said as he settled back against his pillows. "What's been happening around here?"

Patience filled him in on the little things that happened during the week and then she casually brought up the ice cream social that he'd missed.

"Everyone was there," she told him. "Susannah was there, too," she added, testing his reaction.

It irritated her when he immediately perked up. "So. . . how is she doing? Was she there with anyone?" he asked, trying, but failing in his act of nonchalance.

Patience stifled a sigh. "Oh, she's fine. Just fine." She fiddled with the pleats in her skirt. "She didn't come with anyone to the social, but I did see her talking a lot to Bobby Joe Aaron."

His eyes narrowed. "Oh, really."

She nodded, looking out toward the small window, just beyond his bed. "Yes. They're related, you know."

He immediately looked relieved. "Related? I didn't know that. I didn't even know that they knew each other."

She shrugged. "Well, I guess that they're not really related. I mean, she was his late wife's sister."

"Oh." His shoulders slumped and Patience realized how much he liked Susannah.

Was it worth it? Was it worth trying to get the attention of a man who clearly preferred someone else? At first she'd only been attracted to him because there weren't many bachelors around Springton. No good Christian men, anyway. He just seemed like good husband material.

But now, after spending so much time with him, Patience's reasons for liking him had changed.

He had a fine quality about him. But more than that, there was something about him that seemed to reach out to her and speak to her woman's heart. She loved to hear him laugh. She loved to sit and talk with him. Everything about him was interesting and attractive to her.

Patience knew that he liked talking to her, but she was also smart enough to realize that he felt no attraction to her as a woman. He treated her as if she was his little sister or his pal. Would that ever change? Or would she have to be content with being only his friend and watch him as he courted Susannah Butler or some other woman?

Looking at him now, seeing the concern that he had for Susannah, Patience couldn't bring herself to give up. This was too important. He was becoming too important to her.

She couldn't give up. Not yet.

"You know, I never heard Billy Aaron speak of even

knowing Susannah," Lee told her, breaking into her thoughts.

Patience puzzled over that little bit of information. "Hmm. That's strange. When I talked to her she acted like. . ."

"You talked to her?" he interrupted.

"Yesterday, I went. . .I mean. . .uh. . ." Patience stammered, realizing what she just said and mentally kicking herself for the slip.

"What a minute. You saw her yesterday? Where?" he demanded.

Patience looked at his suspicious face and sighed. "I went to her house."

"You *what*?"

Patience jumped up from her seat and started pacing about the room. "I went to her house. Is that a crime?" she asked throwing up her arms dramatically.

He opened his mouth, then shut it. "Well, no. It just seems strange that you would go there. I didn't know you were acquainted," he finished lamely.

"Why should you know? I don't remember us being acquainted until you fainted at my feet!"

"I did not faint! I passed out!"

Patience rolled her eyes. "Thank you for clarifying that!"

But Lee was not to be deterred. "Why did you go to Susannah's house, Patience?" he asked once again.

Patience's mind raced. She couldn't tell him the real reason. But she couldn't lie, either. So she compromised. "I just went to get to know her. She is new in town, you know."

Lee stared at her for a moment. "You just suddenly got the urge to befriend her yesterday?" he asked, unconvinced.

Patience pulled up an innocent face. At least, she hoped it looked innocent. "Yes. Do you have a problem with that?"

Lee sighed. It just took too much effort and energy to understand this woman. He knew there had to be more to this visit with Susannah, and he just hoped that she wasn't trying to sabotage his chance for a relationship with the pretty teacher.

Then he felt bad for thinking ill of Patience. She didn't seem like a spiteful person, and he knew that he shouldn't judge her.

"Well," he said finally, "I guess I'll try getting up and getting dressed today. I feel much better." He slowly got out of bed and for the first time, he didn't feel lightheaded.

Patience rushed over to him. "Be careful, Sheriff!" she admonished. "Maybe you're rushing it."

Lee put his hand out, stopping her words. "Miss Patience, I'm doing fine. I'm feelin' plenty good enough to take care of myself." He smiled at her, flexing his arms out. "You and your mother have done a good job taking care of me, and I know you must be anxious to get me out of your hair."

Patience felt her heart drop to her toes. He was leaving? So soon? Logically she knew that he'd have to leave sooner or later, but she was hoping that it would be much later. She needed more time to figure out what he wanted in a woman. She needed more time for him to get to know her and she, him.

What would Emma Hadley do? What would she say at a time like this?

Patience thought for a minute and suddenly got a wonderful idea.

"You have been no trouble at all, Sheriff. But I'm sure you know what's best for you," she said happily. She went to the tall pine armoire and opened it up. Carefully she took out the clothes that he'd arrived in, all freshly laundered. "Here you go." She handed the clothes over to him.

Patience noticed that Lee looked relieved that she wasn't making a fuss about it. Obviously, he was expecting her to do that very thing.

He took the bundle and nodded to her. "Thank you," he said, his voice holding a question, as if he was unsure of what she was about.

"I'm sure you're anxious to get back to keeping all of Springton safe and sound!" she said briskly as she picked up the tray of dishes. "I'll just let you get ready."

She walked toward the door, and he called after her, "Uh. . .yeah. Well, thanks."

When she got to the door, she paused and turned to Lee. He was standing there, poor man, like he was waiting for the next shoe to fall.

And it did.

"Oh, by the way," she began. "I wouldn't think of letting you fend for yourself while you are getting your strength back. I'll be bringing meals to your work and your house, so that you won't have to worry about all that." She waved her hand airily about and with a pert smile, she left, closing the door behind her.

As usual, he felt emotionally drained when Patience left the room. Talking to her was like being on a boat during a storm—tossed up and down and left feeling dizzy in the end!

He was sure that she was up to something, but what? Surely she wasn't using the meals just to get close to him!

He did have to eat, and heaven knew he'd rather eat someone else's cooking than his own.

He shrugged and proceeded to dress himself. It would be good getting back to his house. He lived on a moderate-sized piece of land outside of Springton in a small house he'd built himself. It wasn't much, consisting of just two bedrooms, a living room, and a kitchen, but he had plans to build on to it. His father and brother had come up to help him and they'd made it sturdy.

But as small as it was, it still felt too big to live there all by himself.

Suddenly a picture of Patience filled his mind. She was standing out on his little white porch. He shook his head and wiped his eyes. He really was going to have to stop doing that! Why was he constantly thinking about her?

It must have been because he was in her house and constantly seeing her. At least it made him feel better to think that!

It was definitely time to go home!

❧

When Patience took the tray to the kitchen, her mother was standing there waiting for her. She didn't look happy.

"Patience Primrose, it's already nine o'clock and not one of your chores is done. This farm doesn't run itself, you know. If you would spend less time mooning over the sheriff and reading that worthless book that you've always got your nose stuck in, maybe we could get things done." She folded her arms under her bosom and narrowed her eyes at her daughter. "And I hate to say it, but you're making a fool of yourself over that man. Practically throwing yourself at him! He's not unconscious anymore, and it's unseemly for you to be in his room for the length of time that you've been spending in there!"

Patience lowered her head, shamefaced. "But, Mama, I didn't mean anything by talking to him, and I'm not *throwing* myself at him," she defended, though it came out weak. She always had a hard time standing up to her mother.

Prudence just shook her head and started rinsing out Lee's dishes. Patience stared pensively at her mother. She needed desperately to talk to another woman about what she was feeling, but she didn't know how her mother would respond.

"Uh. . .Mama?" she began. "Could I talk to you about something?"

Prudence sighed impatiently, but didn't stop what she was doing. "Mercy, girl. All you do is yap! What is it now?"

Patience bit her lip and looked down at her clinched hands. "How does a woman go about getting a young man's attention? I mean, how did you and Papa meet? Did you like him before he liked—"

The dishes crashing in the sink stopped Patience from continuing. Prudence whirled around, her face white. "I don't want to talk about that, you hear? Ever! You just leave it to the Lord to find you a man. Chasing after one don't bring nothing but trouble, you hear? Trouble!"

With that, Prudence stomped out of the house.

Shocked, Patience stood staring at the door. What had she said that was so wrong? All she'd mentioned was her papa.

Slowly Patience sat down at the kitchen table, her mind racing. For as long as Patience could remember, they'd never really talked about her father. When she was little, she remembered her mother saying that he'd died and that had been it!

What was it about her papa that got her mother so upset? Had he been a mean man? Did they not get along?

Patience pushed a stray hair from her face and looked longingly at Lee's bedroom door. Was her mother right? Should she just wait on God to send her the right person? But what if God wanted Lee for her, but he was just being too stubborn to realize it?

No. She must persevere! And she must keep trying to become the woman that Lee wants!

five

A winter chill was in the air as Patience drove Lee back to his house. Patience guided the wagon with the ease of one who'd been handling a team of horses for a long time.

It was late October, and though summer had lasted way into September, it was now staying cool throughout the day. They passed several homesteads and farms on their way to his house. A lot of the trees had been cut down and cleared for farming or grazing. But between the clearings, the oak trees stood tall, their leaves painting the skyline in several shades of gold and orange. And, of course, there were the pines. The smell of them tickled her senses like a gentle perfume.

It was the smell of home and she would never tire of it.

But her attention was not on the trees or the way they smelled. It was on Lee and the fact that she would miss him being with her every minute.

Thank goodness, their ride was not a short one!

Lee's homestead was located not more than four miles from her mother's, but because of how the roadways were laid out between properties, they ended up having to drive twice that far. So far their conversation had consisted of the weather and the scenery.

It wasn't what Patience had in mind at all when she suggested that she be the one to drive him instead of getting Billy Aaron to do it. Somehow she'd pictured a romantic ride where he'd suggest that, because of the chill, she move closer to him. She could almost see them all cuddled up and talking intimately.

So far, when she'd told him that she was chilly, he'd taken off his jacket and handed it to her. When she protested that he might catch a chill, he told her that the cold didn't affect him that much.

Patience sighed. This was not going the way she'd imagined it. Nothing ever did when dealing with the sheriff of Springton!

She discreetly peered at him from the corner of her eye. He was looking out over the land and smiling. She watched as he took a deep breath, breathing the clean, crisp air and then let out a contented sigh.

Her heart started beating a little faster as she looked at him. It wasn't only because he was a handsome man, but that he had a confidence about him. A demeanor that implied that he was happy with his life and his world. He just had to be the most perfect man she'd ever encountered. She wondered if Emma Hadley had ever encountered such a man, and if she had, would she even have been able to capture his affection?

She looked ahead and saw his little white house far in the distance. "Oh! Isn't that where you live?" Of course, she knew that it was his house, but she didn't want him to think that she knew *everything* about him.

He nodded and, for the first time, looked her way. He opened his mouth to say something, but nothing came out. He had the strangest look on his face.

What *was* he thinking?

Lee knew exactly what he was thinking; he just couldn't believe he was thinking it.

He'd turned to tell Patience about his land, when he'd

looked at her and noticed that the wind has loosened several curly strands of her hair and her cheeks were rosy from the chill. But it was her eyes that caught his attention. They were a brilliant, light blue that seemed to light up her whole face.

She was lovely.

Confused, he hastily looked away.

"Were you going to say something?" Patience asked him.

He took a breath and decided that he was cold and must have been hallucinating. "I was just going to say that I hope Billy Ray did a good job of feeding my livestock while I was gone."

She looked at him a second and then nodded. "I'm sure that he did. You know Billy is always proud to do something for you."

Glad to have his mind on something else besides her, he chuckled. "He's a good man. I know that he'd like nothing better than to be a full-time lawman himself. But Bobby Joe would never let him go without making him feel guilty about not sticking with the family business." He took a deep breath while looking over the horizon. "I just wish that Bobby Joe would loosen up, you know? Daniel and Tommy give him plenty of help."

Patience was silent for a moment. "Have you tried to talk to him?"

This time Lee's laughter contained no humor. "I've talked and talked 'til I'm blue in the face. It's almost as if Bobby Joe's life is so miserable he wants to make everyone else feel that way, too."

"That is such a sad story about his wife. I mean, first she runs away, leaving a daughter behind, then only a few weeks later, we hear that she died—from what, no one seems to know. I can't imagine what that poor man is going through. Bobby Joe was so different back then, when he first got married. They'd both seemed so happy. How can a marriage just break up like that? What would make her leave?" Patience asked.

That question disturbed Lee a great deal. He had just arrived in town when the scandal of Bobby Joe's wife leaving hit Springton. And since he'd decided that he would like to get married and have a family, he worried that the same thing could happen to him. He knew that it was important that, whomever he married, God be the center of the relationship. Since he'd made a new commitment to Christ several months ago, he was striving to get his life in order and be the kind of man God would like him to be. It wasn't easy, but the rewards of living for Christ were so great.

He finally answered her. "I don't know, Miss Patience. I do know that Bobby Joe has pulled away from the Lord. If a couple doesn't pray together and trust God together, I believe that they won't have a firm foundation for their marriage. I know that when I turned away from the Lord, my life didn't have the meaning that it does now that I'm walking with Him."

"I agree. Sometimes, God has been all I've had. If I didn't have Him to turn to, I don't know what I would do."

That sentence struck Lee as odd. He turned and looked at her and was puzzled by the wistful expression on her face. "What do you mean, Miss Patience?" he had to ask.

Immediately, she stiffened as if realizing that she'd spoken aloud. "Nothing. I was just talking," she quickly said with a shrug, dismissing it as nothing.

But Lee had a feeling that there *was* something more to

her words. He assumed that since Patience had grown up in Springton that she had plenty of friends that she could turn to. And then there was her mother. But as soon as Lee thought it, he mentally took two steps back. No, her mother wasn't the kind of woman a daughter could confide in. In fact, Lee had never met such a harsh, judgmental person. *What must it be like to live with her?*

They finally reached the road that led to his house. Lee focused his attention on his surroundings.

It really felt good to be home.

❧

When they had stopped in front of his house, Lee climbed down from the wagon and started to tell Patience goodbye. But when she looked at him and smiled sadly, he stopped.

"I hope that you will take care of yourself, Sheriff. It's been nice getting to know you," she told him sincerely.

He opened his mouth again to answer her, but what came out wasn't what he'd intended. "Why don't you come in while I fix us a cup of coffee. Maybe it'll warm you up for your trip back."

Her face lost its sad expression and brightened as she smiled. "That would be mighty nice, Sheriff," she gushed enthusiastically.

He mentally gave himself a kick for the hopeful look that he'd just put on her face. He'd promised himself that he wouldn't encourage her, and here he was inviting her into his house! What was wrong with him?

He smiled halfheartedly and then reached up to help her from the wagon. He put his hands at her waist, and he couldn't help but marvel at how small she was. Deciding to concentrate on the task at hand, he lifted her to the ground.

She braced her hands on his chest to get her balance.

The moment her hands touched him, he felt a stream of warmth run through his body. Shocked, he looked at her and into her bright eyes and unconsciously tightened his grip on her waist.

He felt strange, almost mesmerized, as they stared at each other. She seemed as taken aback as he.

❧

Patience felt as though she couldn't catch her breath. The moment Lee put his hands on her waist, she became more aware of him than she'd ever been before.

She flexed her fingers on his chest and could feel the warmth of his skin beneath his cotton shirt. His face was so close to her own, she could almost imagine him leaning closer and kissing her.

What would it feel like to be kissed by this wonderful man?

She saw that his eyes were growing wider, and much to her embarrassment, she realized that she was beginning to lean closer to him.

Quickly, he let her go and stepped several steps away from her.

"Uh. . . We'd better get on in before we freeze!" he muttered and clumsily turned and ran up his steps to his door.

Patience didn't move at first. She took a deep breath and willed her cheeks to return to their natural color instead of the blaring red she knew they must be. What he must think of her! She'd practically leaned over and kissed him. Patience had never been more embarrassed in her life.

Taking a fortified breath, she straightened her shoulders, walked up the steps and through the door that he was holding open for her. She looked at him as she passed him, but Lee didn't look up.

When she entered the house, she was surprised at how neat the house was. There weren't any signs of frills or ruffles, but it was neatly decorated in a clean style a man would choose. The curtains on the windows were a pretty blue color that matched the pillows on the beige couch. Above the fireplace was a pretty landscape painting with several small pictures placed on the mantel. She guessed that they were of his family.

"You have a nice home," she commented, hoping to break their awkward silence.

He came up behind her, but not too close. "Thanks. My brother and father came up to help me build it a couple of years ago."

She turned and gave him what she hoped was a bright smile. "Where do your brother and father live?"

"Right outside of Houston on the Lazy C Ranch with my mama. My brother helps him run it, but I never was interested in the ranching business. From the time I knew what a sheriff was, I wanted to be one. I'm just glad that my parents understood," he explained.

"Which is why you understand Billy's situation," she surmised.

His grin was sheepish. "Yeah, I guess you're right." He ran a hand through his hair and glanced about the room. "Well, let me go and get that coffee made."

"No," she said stopping him. "I'll go make it. You just sit down and relax. I can find everything."

By the weary look on his face and the slump of his shoulders, she knew that she'd guessed correctly. He merely nodded and sat down on the couch.

She went into the kitchen and tried not to dream that this could be *her* kitchen.

❧

Lee was clearly tired, so she didn't stay long. He walked her to the door and on the way grabbed up his jacket that she'd draped over a chair.

"Here. Put this on. You can return it to me later," he offered, holding the coat open for her.

She nervously turned her back to him so that he could drape it around her back. Was it her imagination or did his hands linger on her shoulders longer than they should have?

But she dismissed that thought. Of course not. He only regarded her as a friend or. . .a sister! He practically ran off when he thought that she might kiss him, didn't he?

She turned back to him and smiled. "I put the hamper of food I brought in your pantry. If you need anything, just let us know."

He nodded. "I will. Thanks. You be careful riding home."

She stared at him a minute more, then turned and walked out to her wagon. She noticed that he watched at the door while she climbed into the buggy and rode out of sight.

What was he thinking?

Lee was thinking about the fact that he'd almost kissed her! He couldn't get over the feeling that had swept over him when they'd been standing close. For that moment, it had felt good to have his hands on her waist and her hands on his chest. He'd wanted nothing more than to reach down and brush her lips with his own. It had seemed right somehow.

Lee shook his head as if trying to clear it. It was the

close proximity to her that was making him confused. It had to be. Now that he was home, things could get back to normal. He could start concentrating his efforts on courting the woman that he really wanted—Susannah Butler.

She was the woman for him. Beautiful, gentle, and graceful. Just the kind of woman a man needed to come home to after a hard day at work. He would never get tired of looking at her. That was for sure.

And while it was true that he hadn't had much time to talk to her, he was sure that they would have a lot in common.

Patience wasn't the only woman that he could talk to!

Tomorrow. Tomorrow he would go and pay her a visit. That surely would get his mind off of Patience Primrose and back on the right track of rational thinking!

six

Getting motivated to get out of bed and go to work wasn't an easy chore, as Lee found out the next morning. His mind was raring to go and get things done, but his body was moaning and groaning for him to stay put.

When his hungry animals started protesting, he finally got up. "All right, all right," he grumbled as he slowly got dressed.

His livestock consisted of three horses and five head of cattle. Just enough to meet his needs and not be a bother to care for. There wasn't a whole lot of crime to deal with in a small town like Springton, but what little there was kept him busy. He didn't want to have to spend his extra time and money trying to run a large spread, too.

With the feeding done, he made his way into town and to the jailhouse, which also contained his office and two jail cells. It was empty when he arrived, so he got to sit and catch his breath for a few minutes.

He didn't get to rest for long, although the man who walked through his door was a welcome interruption.

"Preacher!" Lee greeted the town's minister with a grin. "How's married life?"

The two men shook hands, and Caleb Stone sat in the chair in front of the desk.

"Married life is wonderful. You should try it some time," Caleb answered, a satisfied gleam in his eye.

Lee laughed. "I don't know. I might think about it one

of these days. When did you get back?"

Caleb lifted his hat off his head and ran his fingers through his messy black tresses. "Last night. We were going to come in today, but Rachel was anxious about the kids. I was sorta missing the little boogers myself! I'm just glad that we got someone to run the orphanage for us so we didn't have that worry." He stopped and stared at Lee, his gaze, as always, keen. "You doing all right, Lee? You still don't look that good."

Lee gave his friend a wry grin. "Thanks, Preacher."

Caleb didn't smile. "Are you sure that you should be back at work so soon?"

Lee waved off his concern. "Doc says I'm fine. I just don't have all my strength back, is all."

Caleb studied him a minute more and seemed satisfied. He nodded and then a teasing smile lit his face. "So. . .did Patience Primrose get you all taken care of?"

Lee eyed him warily. "Yeah, she and her mother did all right," he said.

Caleb nodded and pretended to have great interest in his hat. "Hmmm. . . And how was Patience? Did you two get along?"

"What do you mean?"

"I was just wondering if your feelings had changed any where Patience is concerned. I mean, living with someone for nearly a week can bring a whole new perspective to things. And she is sweet on ya. . ."

"No!" Lee immediately denied. Upon seeing Caleb's eyebrows raised in question at Lee's vehement denial, he cleared his throat and spoke more calmly. "Patience is a nice girl, but we're just friends. I made that clear to her."

"Ya did, did ya? So no more batting her eyelashes and

giggling?" Caleb asked. "She got the point that you're not interested?"

Lee glowered at the preacher. "You know good and well she ain't easy to convince. You had to get engaged to someone else before she got the point!"

"So what are you going to do? Get yourself engaged?"

Lee smiled. "I'm working on it."

That got his attention. Caleb popped forward in his chair. "You're what?"

Lee leaned back. "I said I'm working on it. Been thinking 'bout courtin' that new schoolteacher, Susannah Butler."

Caleb thought for a moment. "Isn't she Bobby Joe Aaron's sister-in-law?"

"That's what I heard," Lee said with a shrug. "Anyway, I was supposed to go to the ice cream social with her before I got sick. Thought I'd ask her to a picnic this Saturday."

"Sounds like you got this thing all figured out."

Lee smiled smugly. "I've got a plan, if that's what you're asking." He looked at Caleb more seriously, and then told him what had been on his heart recently. "Lately, I've really been praying that God would send me the perfect mate, like He did for you. I really want to do God's will."

"Then I'll be in prayer for you also," Caleb told him, but then paused. "You know, Lee, what you may think is God's will for you may not be right at all. And then, sometimes what we would never consider in our own minds may be what God wants for us."

"What are you saying?" Lee asked, confused.

Caleb took a breath and shook his head. "I don't know.

I just felt God wanted me to tell you that."

Lee groaned and ran his hand over his face. "Don't do that to me, Preacher. You can't just throw something out there and not explain it!"

"A little mystery in your life is good, Sheriff. I don't make up these little insights; I just deliver them," he said with a shrug. Then he laughed. "Maybe if you didn't have all these women troubles, you'd be able to hear Him for yourself."

At that moment, Patience breezed into the office. "Why hello, you all!" she said in a strange accent.

Caleb glanced at Lee and then turned in his chair to face Patience. "Been down South lately, Miss Patience?" he asked, as if quite amused.

"Why no, Brother Caleb," she answered and quickly changed the subject. "You all are back from your honeymoon?"

Caleb nodded. "Yes, I was just telling Lee here that the married life was something he should experience for himself."

Lee stopped himself from rolling his eyes. He was getting paid back for all the times that he teased the preacher when Patience had shown interest in him! He could practically see the marriage-minded wheels in Patience's head spinning.

"You're thinking of getting married, Sheriff?" Patience asked with great interest.

"No!" Lee practically shouted.

Patience's eyebrows lifted and Lee admonished himself for letting all this marriage talk get to him. "I mean, I hope to one day, but I'm not in a big hurry."

Patience smiled at him. "That's the way I feel, Sheriff!"

Lee could tell that Caleb was biting his lip in an attempt not to laugh. Lee gave him a withering glare.

"Seems like you two have something in common," he casually mentioned.

Lee hopped up from his desk. "Didn't you mention that you had something to do, Preacher?" he asked, looking pointedly at Caleb.

This time Caleb chuckled aloud. "Well, if I don't, I'm sure I can find something to do." He got up and donned his hat, tipping it in Patience's direction. "Miss Patience, you have a good morning."

Patience beamed at him. "You, too, Brother Caleb."

They both watched the preacher close the door behind him, and then Patience turned to Lee with a smile. "He seems happy, doesn't he? Marriage must agree with him."

Lee had about all the marriage talk he could take this morning. He *especially* did not want to discuss it with Patience! "Yeah, uh. . .well. Did you need me for something this morning?" he asked briskly.

Patience looked down at the basket and the jacket she'd been holding. "Oh yes! I brought you some muffins. I thought you might not feel like fixing yourself anything, so I made extra for you. And I also wanted to return your jacket and thank you for letting me borrow it last night."

It was the first time he noticed that she had her hands full. It made him feel a little guilty for being so short with her. "I appreciate it, Miss Patience. I was getting a little hungry."

"Well, we surely don't want you to starve!" she exclaimed as she put the basket on his desk, then laid his jacket beside it. She was speaking with an accent once again.

He just had to ask.

"Uh. . .Patience, why do you keep doing that?"

She frowned, but kept laying out the contents of the basket. "Doing what?"

He put his hands on his hips, then let them fall at his side again. "That thing with your voice. You sound. . . funny!"

That got her attention. She looked at him with a strange expression on her face. "I don't know what you mean."

The accent was gone. He narrowed his eyes. "There you go again. Now it's gone."

She giggled nervously. "Really, Sheriff. . . ," she muttered, picking up the basket and hurrying toward the door. "Well, I'll just leave you to your breakfast!"

"You're not going to join me?" he called after her.

She opened the door and plastered a smile on her face as she looked back at him. "No, no. That's okay. Goodbye!" With that she stepped out and shut the door behind her.

Lee chuckled, then laughed out loud. He had to admit, Patience was fun to tease. He never knew what that girl was up to or what she was going to do next!

He sighed happily and sat down, savoring the muffins and the sweet rolls that Patience left behind.

And there was one more thing he liked about Patience.

The woman could cook.

❧

Patience walked over to the bench that sat outside the sheriff's office and slumped down onto it.

What a disaster! She'd practiced all morning on that Southern accent, and all she'd managed to do was to make Lee think she was even more strange.

She bent over, cupped her face in her hands, and groaned. This wasn't going to work. She was an utter failure at this sort of thing. She was going to die an old maid. That was all there was to it!

"Patience?" a sweet Southern voice asked overhead.

Slowly Patience raised her head, and after taking a look at the woman in front of her, she wished that she'd never looked up. What she didn't need was to see her competition looking more beautiful than ever.

Patience pulled her eyes away from the radiant pink-striped gown—Redheads weren't supposed to look good in pink, were they?—and then looked down at her own plain, beige dress.

Forget the accent, Patience thought, *I need new clothes!*

She made a mental note to think on that later and looked back up at Susannah. "Hi, Miss Butler. How are you?" she greeted.

Susannah smiled and sat down beside her. A wave of honeysuckle drifted over to Patience, as the pretty woman straightened the frills and ruffles on her skirt.

"I'm so glad I ran into you!" she began. "I surely did want to thank you for that dee-licious pie you brought to my house."

Susannah was so nice, it was hard not to respond to her enthusiasm. "You're welcome, Susannah. I'm glad you liked it."

"I also wanted to ask you if you would come to dinner at my house tomorrow night. I'm just having a few people over that I've met in the short time I've been here. You know, so that I can get to know everybody a little better. It'll just be the pastor and his new wife and Bobby Joe, if he'll come, and his brother, Billy. Oh, and I plan on asking Sheriff Cutler. That's where I was just headed."

Patience's heart dropped. "The sheriff, huh?"

"Oh yes," Susannah gushed. "Isn't he a handsome man? Those golden eyes of his can just make a girl's heart go all aflutter! And I heard that you took care of him! Wasn't that just sweet of you! I do hope that he's recovering nicely."

Patience didn't know when she'd felt so depressed. Susannah thought Lee was handsome. It was clear that she was attracted to him. And with Lee reciprocating those feelings, where did that leave Patience?

Home alone with Mama for the rest of her life. That's where. It was a depressing thought.

"He's doing fine. He's in his office. I just came from there," Patience answered faintly.

Susannah beamed. "Oh, good! Well, I'll just run in there and ask him if he'll come." She hopped up and tugged at her little pink gloves. "Can I count on your being there?"

Patience knew that she shouldn't go. It would be humiliating to be in the presence of this woman and the pretty preacher's wife, Rachel. She would look so plain in comparison. But she didn't want to leave Lee alone with this Southern beauty, either. "I'll be there," she answered.

"All righty. I'll see you around six tomorrow?"

Patience nodded and with a friendly wave good-bye, Susannah let herself into the sheriff's office.

Staring after her, Patience felt envious. Susannah had everything that Patience wished that she had. What chance did she have if Susannah truly did want Lee for herself?

Patience turned away and looked down the street. She

couldn't let herself think like that. The feelings that Patience had for the sheriff had become something strong and powerful in the days that she'd gotten to know him. To think that he'd never be hers was more than she could handle at that moment.

There had to be a way.

She got up and took another look down at her dress. *Clothes.* She needed to do something about her clothes. But what?

She looked down the street and saw the sign of the mercantile swinging in the wind. She wrapped her woolen shawl tightly around her and made her way in that direction.

seven

When his office door opened once again, Lee didn't even look up. He just assumed that he knew who it was—Patience. "I really do need to get some work done, here," he said firmly and kept on writing.

"Oh! Well, I promise I won't take up much of your time, Sheriff," a musical Southern voice answered.

Lee's head popped up and he was greeted with the lovely presence of Miss Susannah Butler. "I'm sorry I was so rude," he said quickly. "I thought you were. . . uh. . .someone else," he finished lamely.

She seemed to float across the room to where he sat. At the last minute, Lee remembered his manners and jumped up from his seat and motioned toward the empty chair. "Won't you have a seat?" he offered politely.

"Why, thank you." She sat in a puffy cloud of striped pink and white and proceeded to pull off her dainty gloves. "I just wanted to stop by and invite you to a dinner party at my house tomorrow night. I'm only inviting a handful of people, just those I've become acquainted with recently. I would be most honored if you'd be counted among my guests," she implored with a sweet smile.

He looked at her for a moment and blinked, amazed that she hadn't even taken a breath during her whole speech. "Well, sure! I can be there. What time?"

She clasped her hands together in an apparent show of joy. "Oh, that's wonderful! Everyone is arriving at six.

And don't worry about bringing anything—I'm cooking plenty of everything. I also invited Billy and Bobby Joe, too; though I don't think that Bobby Joe will come. He's such a stubborn old thing. And Daniel and Tommy can't come because they are out of town, but I did invite the preacher and his wife and they said that they would be happy to come. Oh, and I almost forgot, I also invited. . ."

The door opened and Lee couldn't help but take a breath of relief that someone had interrupted her. Had she talked so much before? He couldn't remember that. Maybe he'd found it irritating because he was feeling so poorly and weak. That had to be it.

Texas Ranger Gene Brown stepped into the office, dragging a cuffed, scruffy-looking man behind him. "Lee! Glad to see that you're out and about. Unfortunately I've got a present for you," he greeted as he yanked the outlaw to his side.

Susannah, upon seeing the man, jumped up from her seat, clasped her hands to her chest, and gasped aloud. "Mercy!"

Lee was instantly next to her. "Gene, why don't you lock up our guest, there, while I escort Miss Susannah outside," he said as he tossed Gene the keys.

Gene nodded and halfway dragged the man toward the cell.

Lee took Susannah's arm and ushered her outside.

"I'm sorry about that, Miss Susannah. But you never know what's going to come through my office. I mean, it is a jail, too," he explained.

"Oh, don't be a silly-willy, Sheriff. I'm perfectly fine. That poor man just startled me, is all," she said, waving off his concern. She pulled her gloves back on in a smart fashion and gave him a breezy smile. "But that was awfully gallant of you to come to my rescue like that!"

She laid her hand on his arm and smiled at him.

❧

Patience let herself into the mercantile and went directly to the section of the store that she was most interested in. The material.

"Hello, Patience!" Addie Hayes, the store's owner, called out from behind the counter. "What can I do for you today?"

Patience walked up to where she stood and motioned to the shelves behind Mrs. Hayes. "I just wanted to look at your material, Mrs. Hayes. I was thinking about making a new dress."

Addie smiled and then turned and looked at her inventory. "Hmmm, let's see. I have some of that gray cotton that your mother likes so much and, of course, the brown wool if you're looking for warmth. It's October and getting colder everyday!"

But Patience shook her head. "No, I was looking for something. . .prettier?" she explained, her voice uncertain. She scanned the shelves and her eyes lit on the green silk material on the third shelf. "Something like that."

Addie followed to where Patience was pointing and asked, "The green?"

"Yes."

"Now, this is a pretty color!" She pulled it loose and held it against Patience's face. "Oh, and look at that. It just brightens your whole face!"

Patience wasn't expecting the compliment. She blushed. "Do you really think so?"

"It certainly does! You could sew a fancy dress using this material!"

Patience's face fell. "Oh. I'm sorry, Mrs. Hayes. I can't get this. I never have gotten the hang of using a sewing needle. Mama makes all my clothes and she would surely pitch a fit if I brought this material to her to sew. And besides, I don't have enough money for silk," she finished sadly. She let herself touch the pretty silk one last time before she let it go.

Addie studied her for a moment, then nodded her head as if coming to a decision. "You know, Patience, I've had to run things by myself ever since Rachel got married, and it sure is rough on an old woman like me. I don't suppose you would want to help me a few days a week, would you? You could buy all the material you want, then Rachel could sew them for you."

Hope welled within Patience's heart. Did she dare? "But Mrs. Hayes, my mother would have an absolute fit!" she lamented, voicing her worst fear.

Mrs. Hayes rolled her eyes at that. "Oh fiddlesticks! I've dealt with Prudence before. You just leave her to me." She tapped her cheek in contemplation. "In fact, why don't I drop by and ask her myself. It'll sound better coming from me, anyhow."

Patience bit her lower lip and looked down at the beautiful green silk again. She could see herself entering a room wearing the green silk fashioned in a flowing, stylish gown. Lee wouldn't be able to miss her in this color!

She looked back up at Mrs. Hayes. "All right, let's do it!"

Addie laughed, as if she and Prudence had butted heads before and was looking forward to the chance to do it again! "I'll be by around seven this evening."

Patience giggled with excitement. "Okay! See you tonight!" She turned and practically skipped out of the store.

When she ran down the steps, she had visions of beautiful dresses dancing around in her head. She turned to walk to her wagon that was parked by the sheriff's office and froze.

Lee and Susannah were standing closely together, right by her wagon. She had her hand on his arm and they were gazing into each other's eyes.

"Oh no!" she whispered. She tried to swallow, but to her horror, tears began to gather in her eyes.

She blinked furiously, determined that she was not going to let this upset her. She was not going to cry!

"Aren't they just the cutest couple," a high-pitched voice commented.

Patience turned slightly and saw Amy McLain and Jessica Buford standing with their heads together, their attentions fixed on the couple across the street from them. Amy and Jessica were the same age as Patience and had been schoolmates of hers. Both were married to the sons of the town's only banker.

But they had never been Patience's friends.

Jessica giggled. "I'll bet he's thrilled to be out of the Primrose house! Can you imagine having to endure five days with Prudence? And poor, plain Patience couldn't have been much company to him! She's such a mousy thing, isn't she?"

"I'll say," Amy agreed while patting her chestnut curls that were all still perfectly in place, despite the wind. "I can't imagine the poor thing ever finding herself a husband. She'll probably end up an old maid."

Jessica nodded. "Well, we really do need to make Susannah's acquaintance. She seems like someone that we would want to befriend."

Patience's tears were abandoned in favor of anger. How many times in her life had she had to endure the pettiness of girls like those two? Never had they asked her to join in with them or invited her to their parties. When she'd been younger, she'd tried so hard to get them to like her, but they'd just ridiculed her more. Poor plain Patience. So pathetic in her attempts to be in their circle. Never belonging.

She never really belonged anywhere.

And as usual, she let them walk away without saying anything in her own defense. They never even seemed to notice her standing there.

Taking a deep breath, she prayed that God would help her with her anger, then started across the street to her wagon.

❧

Lee returned Susannah's smile and glanced down to where her hand rested on his arm.

But something was wrong. Her smile, while it had dazzled him in the past, didn't do a thing to him today. He'd dreamed of her touch, but there was no spark or warmth now that she actually was touching him. He felt disappointed.

He suddenly thought of last night, when he'd helped Patience from the wagon. Her touch had made him feel more than he cared to admit.

Susannah was the woman he was interested in. Shouldn't her touch have more effect on him?

A movement in his side vision made him look up. Patience, wrapped tightly in her woolen shawl, was coming toward them. She didn't even look up as she walked to her wagon and climbed into it.

He didn't know what made him do it, but he stepped away from Susannah's touch.

"Oh! Hello, Patience!" Susannah called out.

Patience looked at them as if she didn't know they'd been standing there. "Oh, hello, Susannah. . .and you, too, Sheriff."

Lee cocked an eyebrow at her cool voice. "Going home, Miss Patience?"

She noticed, just then, that he'd stepped away from Susannah. That melted her coolness considerably. Maybe she had more of a chance with the sheriff than she'd realized. He'd actually moved away from the fair Susannah to acknowledge her! With a genuine smile, she answered, "Yes, but I'll be back to bring you some lunch, Sheriff."

"I'd be most obliged."

She waved good-bye to them both and rode away.

Susannah watched as the wagon disappeared down the street. "I really like Patience. She's a real sweet girl, don't you think?" she commented.

Lee agreed. "Yes, she is," he murmured thoughtfully.

"Well, I surely hope that we can become fast friends! I could really use one, being that I'm a stranger to this state!"

Lee looked at her curiously. "Aren't you friends with Bobby Joe Aaron and his family?"

Her bright face suddenly darkened. "Not really, although I've tried to be. . ." She tugged her shawl closer around her and changed the subject. "I guess I should say to-di-loo, and I'll see you tomorrow night. Now, don't you forget about the dinner. I just think. . ."

"I won't!" he quickly interjected. "I better get back in and see about that prisoner."

She smiled. "Okay, Sheriff. Good-bye, now."

"Good-bye," he said, and they both turned to go their separate ways.

Lee went back into the office where Gene was waiting for him.

"What's his story?" Lee asked, motioning toward the outlaw, who had already made himself comfortable on the cot inside the cell.

"He and his brother have hit a couple stagecoaches in this area. I brought him to you in hopes that his brother will show up and try to bail him out. I know you are short-handed around here, but I wanted to ask if you could keep a round-the-clock watch while he's here. If we can get his brother, we'll have a much better case. He's wanted in Louisiana, Arkansas, and Texas."

Lee nodded. "I'll see if my deputies can help out."

Gene slapped him on the shoulder. "Good. I'll be checking in." He picked up a paper from Lee's desk. "Here is a picture of his brother. You might want to get them copied and post them around town."

"I'll run them by the newspaper office."

Gene picked up his hat. "Okay! You take care, you hear?"

"Will do," Lee answered.

❧

After Gene had left, Lee sank back down into his chair.

"You can have as many deputies as you want guarding this place. It ain't gonna make no difference. If Otis wants me out, then he'll get me out," the outlaw spoke from his cell.

Lee, not in the mood to deal with the man, wearily rubbed his eyes. "Look. . ." He glanced down at the papers Gene had given him. ". . .Powell. I'm not in the mood to play my-brother-is-tougher-than-yours, all right? Just sit there real quiet-like and we'll get along just fine. I might even let you eat lunch." Then he silently groaned. Lunch! He'd need to make provisions for meals for this wise guy. Then he remembered Patience. Maybe she could run down to the inn and pick something up for him.

"You'll be sorry," the outlaw spoke again.

Lee rolled his head back and looked beseechingly heavenward. "I'm already sorry."

eight

Sheriff Cutler was becoming more and more dear to Patience, and Patience was afraid that she was becoming more and more. . .like a sister to him. Worse than that, she felt she was being a pest!

She'd taken his lunch and had even run down to the inn to get food for his prisoner. He'd seemed glad to get the food, but when she'd suggested she sit with him, he told her that it wasn't necessary. That he was going to work while he ate. In fact, he barely even *looked* at her the whole time she'd been in his office.

She was obviously getting on his nerves. That had to be the problem. But she didn't know how else to get his attention. The only thing that she could come up with was to alter her appearance.

But she needed the mercantile job to accomplish that. And for that, she needed her mama's blessing.

It wasn't soon in coming. Prudence threw an absolute fit!

Patience knew that she would. How could her mother ever understand how Patience felt? Though she'd lived alone all these years, Prudence had once been married and had borne a child. Patience would never have a chance to do any of that unless her mother gave in. She needed the job Addie Hayes offered. It would not only give her extra money for new clothes, it would give her a sense of self-worth.

"My daughter does not have to work like a common laborer! I'll not have it, I tell you. She doesn't get her work done around here as it is."

Addie Hayes folded her arms about her middle and gave Prudence a direct look. "Patience would only be helping me out in the afternoons. There'd be plenty of time to get her chores done around here."

Prudence turned her shrewd gaze toward her daughter. "And why do you want this job? What are you up to, girl?"

Patience forced herself not to cringe from her mother's tone. She bravely stood her ground. "I would like to have my own money, Mama. I'm twenty-one years old and it doesn't look like I'll be getting married. Not yet, anyway. So I want to do this for myself." She braced herself for her mother's harsh words that she knew would probably come.

"All you're going to do is cause folks around here to talk and to speculate about why you have a job! They will think we're hurtin' for money. Is that what you want to do, girl? Bring shame to this house?"

"No. You know that I don't want that, Mama. I just want to make a little money on my own."

"Selfishness! That's all it is!" Then Prudence sharpened her gaze on Addie. "And you! You're sticking your nose where it don't belong! Well, I wash my hands of it!" With that she got up from her chair and walked out of the room.

Embarrassed at her mother's rudeness, Patience hastened to explain. "I'm sorry, Mrs. Hayes. I don't know what's wrong with Mama lately. She's acting awfully strange. I. . ."

Addie waved her words aside. "Oh, you don't have to explain your mama to me. Rachel told me she's going through a lot of things on the inside. You just keep praying for her; she'll be all right."

Patience reached up and smoothed a stray strand of hair from her face and tucked it behind her ear. "I just wish I knew what's wrong with her. I mentioned my father the other day, and she acted like I'd just asked about the devil himself!"

Addie shook her head, confusion marring her brow. "I don't know about that. Never knew your father. Prudence was already widowed when she came to Springton."

"I know. But other than telling me that he'd died before I was born, she's never mentioned him. I guess I'm just curious about who he was." She shrugged. "But I don't reckon that I'll ever know."

Addie reached out and patted Patience on the hand. "Well, don't worry yourself sick over it. Maybe working at the store will get your mind off it. You are old enough to make this decision for yourself, Patience, whether your mama likes it or not."

Patience was thoughtful for a moment. She'd never openly defied her mother before, but she could see the truth in Mrs. Hayes's words. She was a grown-up. It was something her mama would have to learn to accept. She looked up into Addie's eyes and brightened. "I'm really excited about working for you, Mrs. Hayes. I do so want to be able to purchase pretty cloth for new dresses. I've got to do something to attract the sheriff, or I'm afraid that I'm going to end up an old maid!" she wailed.

Addie practically crowed. "Oh, ho! So that's how the wind blows, does it? Well, you just leave it to Rachel and me. We'll get you all prettied up! You just wait and see."

"Oh, Mrs. Hayes. Do you really think you can?"

Addie smiled and arose from her chair. "Yes, I do. Now, let me go so you can go on in and get your beauty rest."

Patience giggled excitedly as she got up and walked her to the door. "I'll see you tomorrow."

Addie waved. "Just be there around nine. That will be fine."

"Okay," Patience answered. "Oh, and Mrs. Hayes?" she called out.

Addie turned and looked back at Patience.

"Thank you."

Addie just smiled and climbed into her buggy.

❧

The boards creaked softly as Lee stepped out onto his little porch and eased his lanky body into the swing. The crickets were out and singing in full chorus; their song had a peaceful effect on Lee as he nudged the swing into a gentle sway.

He'd gotten Billy Aaron to bunk at the jail for the night to keep watch over their prisoner. He really hoped they caught Otis Powell soon. It was hard finding men to volunteer for things like taking the night watch. Lee knew that he'd probably end of up doing most of it himself. He just wished he'd get all his strength back so he'd be up to it when his time came.

But even the singing of the crickets could not wipe away the nagging guilt he was feeling for snubbing Patience today at the office.

He had come to a decision about her, and he was trying his best to carry it through. He'd decided to act cool so that she would stop getting her hopes up about them having any kind of relationship. He saw the expression on her face, the attraction for him that was written in her every look. She was much too sweet a girl to be hurt by his rejection. He had to do it now, before it was too late.

He laid his head back on the swing and stared up at the blue ceiling of his porch. He'd just finished painting it that color because one of the women from church had said that it would stop dirt-daubers from building nests in his eaves. They would see the blue and mistake it for the sky. That's what he was told anyway. He supposed he wouldn't find out till spring.

Spring. . . Would he be married at that time? He figured that he'd go to this party and, afterward, he'd invite Susannah on a picnic the next day. From there they would start dating frequently. Everybody would see them together and start acknowledging them as a couple. At Christmas he could present her with a ring, and by March they could be married.

Lee smiled. It sounded like a good plan to him.

Except. . . Oh, he shouldn't be thinking it. He shouldn't let doubts creep in! Yet he couldn't help but be, well, bored when she started talking on and on, as she tended to do. That was just her vivacious personality, he supposed. But could he live with that for the rest of his life? Why couldn't she just have a normal conversation with him like. . .Patience.

He closed his eyes and grimaced. He wasn't going to think about her anymore! He especially wasn't going to compare her with Susannah.

Patience was his friend. So he guessed it would be okay to think of her that way. It didn't mean anything. It didn't mean that *she* meant anything to him!

He blew out a breath. Why was everything so confusing? He'd been so clear about everything before he ended up in Patience's care. So sure of what he wanted.

Now. . .he wasn't sure about anything.

❧

Patience drove up to Susannah's house at a quarter past six. By the wagons and buggies lined up in Susannah's small yard, Patience could see that most everybody was there. From inside the house came a hum of chatter, peppered with a dash of laughter here and there.

Lee's horse was tied to the only tree in the yard.

He's here.

Patience closed her eyes for a moment, gathering needed strength. She opened them and, with a fortified breath, stepped down from the wagon. Carefully she smoothed the pleats of her best dress and tucked the curly stray strands of her hair back into place.

Her dress was made of a dark blue material that would have been quite attractive. . .on a brunette. On her, it merely made her look paler than usual. And the neck of it was so tall, she felt like she was choking at times. But it was better than anything else she owned. It would simply have to do until she could purchase the green silk.

She walked the few steps to the house and knocked on the door.

Susannah opened it after a few moments and smiled broadly upon seeing her new friend. "Patience! I was just beside myself when six o'clock came and went and you weren't here yet. Please, come on in! I was just about to set supper on the table."

She took Patience's hand and pulled her into the parlor, where the rest of the guests were gathered.

"Looky, you all! Patience did make it, after all!" she announced to the whole room. Then she turned to Patience. "You know Reverend Stone and his wife, of course, and Billy Aaron—his brother didn't come—and over there is Lee."

Patience looked over to where the sheriff stood, conversing with Brother Caleb. But when Susannah said his first name, he lifted his head and his gaze clashed with Patience's.

Lee had been merely curious at hearing his name spoken, but he froze when he saw Patience standing there. He'd heard someone else come in, but he'd been interested in something the preacher was saying and hadn't looked up.

He didn't know that she would be here.

Was there anywhere he could go that Patience Primrose wasn't?

Very politely he nodded to her and turned his gaze back to the preacher, only the preacher was no longer paying attention to him. He was looking at Patience, too. And before Lee could open his mouth to stop him, Caleb was already talking. "Miss Patience! We're glad you're here. Now everything is even. Billy can sit beside Miss Susannah and Lee, here, can escort you to the table."

Lee glared at him and whispered under his breath, "I'll get you for this, Preacher."

Caleb continued to smile as Patience made her way over to where they were.

"Hi, Brother Caleb," she greeted first. She then looked at Lee with a wary expression that made him feel like a complete heel. "And how are you, Sheriff?" she asked sounding tentative.

Lee made himself relax and squelched his irritations. "Hi, Patience. That lunch you fixed today was mighty tasty." Actually he hadn't really tasted it. He'd felt so horrible for treating her coolly that he hadn't felt like eating.

Patience's face lit up prettily. "Oh, thank you, Sheriff! It was my pleasure!" she gushed. The wary look was gone, replaced by a dreamy sort of look.

He'd done it, again. He'd gotten her hopes up.

"Okay, you all! The food's ready, if you all would follow Billy and me into the dining room!" Susannah announced, taking Billy's arm.

Lee watched Susannah precede him into the dining room. The preacher and Rachel were next. That left him and Patience.

Cautiously, he looked sideways at her and saw that she was watching everyone leave the room. She seemed to be waiting for something.

With a sigh, he held out his arm to her. She blushed and carefully reached up and put her arm through his.

Lee felt that touch all the way to his toes.

Shocked, he looked down at her hand, then up to her eyes. She was a tall girl, so it wasn't hard to look directly into her eyes.

She was wearing the same expression he was. She quickly looked away, and her blush blossomed to a deep red hue.

Taking a breath, Lee tried to rationalize why her touch would, once again, make him feel this way, why Susannah, his dream girl, could touch him and he felt no different.

But one tiny little touch from Patience sent his senses reeling.

There had to be an explanation. A logical reason for this.

nine

He ignored her all the way through dinner. Oh, he'd answer her when she asked him a question, but other than one-syllable answers with a less than halfhearted effort, he ignored her.

It was what happened after dinner that Patience would forever remember as the "dessert disaster."

It all started when Susannah announced that she was serving dessert. Patience remembered a passage from Miss Emma Hadley's book about the eloquence of serving: "A young man's head is easily turned when presented with a young woman who shows elegance and refinement in the way she serves a table."

So Patience hopped up immediately and offered her assistance. It was going so well. She first served Billy, carefully pouring his coffee and then gracefully setting his plate of chocolate cake in front of him.

Then she got to Lee. Once she'd served his coffee and cake, she felt so proud of herself that she'd looked at him and smiled.

Her eyes met his. She smiled brighter. He, staring at her as if mesmerized, smiled back. And then. . .*it* happened.

She fell flat on her back!

She'd liked to think that there had been a reason for her to trip. But, in fact, it had been nothing but clumsiness. She'd been so overwhelmed that he'd smiled at her, that she'd stepped back. The heel of her shoe had gotten caught in the hem of her dress. And the next thing she knew, she was on the floor, staring at the ceiling.

She sat up and that was when she noticed everybody's reaction. Susannah gasped and came right over to her. Billy looked shock. The preacher stood up, looking concerned. Rachel put her hand over her own heart and asked if Patience was all right.

But it was the sheriff's reaction that really upset her.

He laughed.

And he laughed. In fact, the nitwit couldn't stop laughing!

Susannah helped her up and began fussing over her dress. "Oh, you *poor* thang! I am *so* sorry that something like this has happened. I should have insisted on getting the dessert myself. I just feel plumb awful, is what I feel! I. . ."

Patience put her hand out. "It's all right, Susannah," she interrupted. "Really, I'm fine."

At once, everybody started gathering around her, helping her to her chair and picking up the few utensils she'd dropped. But the laughter coming from the chair beside her could not be ignored.

Rachel, ever mindful of others' feelings, spoke up. "Really, Sheriff. It's not very nice to laugh at her. Patience could have been really hurt."

Lee made a show of trying to stop, but failed. "I'm sorry, Patience, I really am. It's. . . ," he laughed again, "that I. . . ," another outburst of the rude sound, "can't seem to stop!"

Tears filled Patience's eyes, though she tried very hard to keep them at bay. "Um. . .I think that I will go now. It is getting late," she said, quickly standing up.

She deliberately turned her back to Lee, not wanting him to see her tears.

Susannah looked crestfallen. "Oh, Patience. Please don't cry. Did you hurt yourself, after all?" she asked innocently, but Patience wished she could have just been quiet.

"I really need to go," she answered and walked briskly to the parlor to get her shawl. That was when she made her decision. She'd taken enough teasing in her life to know when something was pointless. And a relationship with Leander Cutler was just that. She was going to leave the man alone.

❧

Patience's leaving and Susannah's mentioning the girl's tears put an abrupt stop to Lee's laughter. He honestly didn't know what had happened to him to make him laugh. He supposed that it was that he and Patience had become such good friends that he treated her as he would have if it had been any of his friends who'd ended up all sprawled on the floor. He laughed.

But now he knew that he'd been wrong. Terribly wrong. He'd made her cry. He felt like such a heel.

He got up to go to her, but Rachel stopped him.

"I know that you didn't mean to, Lee, but you've hurt her feelings. I think you are the last person she needs to see right now," Rachel told him.

Lee felt the sting of her words all the way to his gut. Now more than ever he wanted to make things right with her. But he nodded reluctantly. "All right, Rachel. But please tell her I'm as sorry as I can be."

Rachel told him she would and hurried from the room.

She caught up with Patience just as she was climbing onto her wagon.

"Patience, wait!"

Patience gripped the hard wood rail on the wagon and closed her eyes. Why couldn't she have been faster? She didn't want to talk to Rachel, or anyone, for that matter. She just wanted to be left alone and find a quiet spot to have a good cry.

But Rachel could not be ignored. For one, she was the pastor's wife. Two, she was too nice, and Patience knew that she was just trying to help.

So, she quickly dried her tears and slowly turned and stepped back off of the wagon. "I'm okay, Rachel," she told her, trying, but failing, to sound brave.

Rachel walked up to her, her eyes shining with compassion. "No. You're not okay, Patience. I know that Lee hurt your feelings in there." Patience started to disagree, but Rachel went on. "And I know how much you like him."

Patience looked at her with dismay. "You do? Oh, *great!*" She threw up her hands. "I suppose the whole town knows that I am making a fool of myself over him."

Rachel reached out and took her hand. "I know because Caleb told me. He saw how you looked at Lee at his office the other day. He's seen that same look on my face, Patience. That's all."

Patience looked down at her hands and thought fleetingly that she had never had a friend to talk to, a friend who would offer her comfort. But here Rachel was, offering just that. Patience slowly raised her eyes to the pretty woman. "I don't know what I'm going to do, Rachel. When it started, I just figured he'd make a good husband.

But now. . .now it's different. I can't explain it," she said with a frustrated shake of her head.

Rachel squeezed her hand. "You don't have to. I know what it's like to love a man you think you could never have. Even to want a life that seems impossible."

A tear rolled down Patience's pale cheek. "But look at you, Rachel. You are so beautiful, and Brother Caleb loved you from the beginning. And now look at me." She let go of Rachel's hand and held her arms out on either side of her. "Sheriff Cutler won't even *consider* that I'm courtin' material! He looks right past my plain face and latches on to Susannah's pretty one. Why couldn't I just be someone else? Someone who he could love," she wailed and slumped against her wagon, burying her head in her hands.

"That's the biggest bunch of self-pity I've heard in a long time!"

"What?" Patience's head snapped up at Rachel's scornful tone.

Rachel put her hands on her hips and made a "tsk"ing noise. "I'll admit, I said the same thing plenty of times after I was molested and after the church rejected me. But to wish that you were someone other than what God created you to be is just like telling God that He made a mistake when He made you!"

Patience blinked. "But. . .well I. . . ," she started and stopped. Then she sighed. "You're right."

Rachel nodded. "Of course, I'm right! Now, Addie told me that you were going to start working for her tomorrow." After Patience nodded her head, she continued, "Well, I'm going to get sewing on that new dress you wanted, and we're also going to get to working on *you*!"

Patience felt a little dizzy. "Me?"

"Yes, you. I didn't say that God didn't give us the good sense to work with what we have. Sometimes we just need to do a little polishing!"

"Okay," she answered, though she hadn't a clue as to what Rachel was talking about.

"Be at my house right after you get off of work, and I'll tell you what we're going to do!" Rachel all but ordered.

"Okay," Patience answered again.

Rachel smiled broadly. "Well, then! I'll let you get on back home! You be careful!" And with that, Mrs. Rachel Stone sashayed back into the house, leaving Patience bewildered and excited all at the same time.

❧

"You look worried, Lee," Susannah said from behind him. He was standing at her window and watching as Patience rode away.

Lee turned and schooled his features to a pleasant expression. He didn't want her getting the idea that he had feelings for Patience. Not when he needed to get onto the business of courting her!

"I just feel bad for hurting her feelings. I didn't mean to laugh at her. Patience and I have become friends, and I didn't think she would mind," he said with a shrug.

Susannah wrung her hands. "I do hope she is all right."

Lee looked back to the window. "Patience is a good sport. She'll be okay." He had to believe that. He could not dwell on her anymore. He had to get down to the business at hand.

Courting business.

"Uh. . .Susannah, I wanted to ask you something." He turned once again to face her.

Susannah smiled and linked her arm through his, leading him back to the dining room. "Ask away, Sheriff!"

He took a deep breath. "Would you like to take a stroll with me down by the stream tomorrow?"

Susannah twirled around, facing him, and laid a hand on his arm. "Oh, that would be delightful, Sheriff! What time shall we go?"

"Around noon? I'll drop by and pick you up."

❧

Patience was halfway home when her wagon wheel broke. Stunned, she looked over the flickering ears of her horses, then bent to peer over the side.

Broken.

Patience blew out a frustrated breath as she straightened and looked around in the moonlight, trying to get her bearings.

She was by the Aaron brothers' sawmill. Good. The brothers lived in a big house beside the mill. Surely they could help her.

She was climbing out of the wagon when she remembered something she'd heard at the party. Daniel and Tommy were out of town and Billy was still at Susannah's. She couldn't remember what had been said about Bobby Joe. She hoped that he was home.

The wind was getting colder, and Patience's thin wrap wasn't enough protection from the biting weather. Carefully she stepped onto the dirt road and searched through the darkness for the cutoff that led to their house.

She found it and also found something else—the row of shacks that housed a lot of the workers from the mill.

Instantly, Patience became frightened. Most were decent, but she'd heard tell that they liked to drink at night. Mama had always warned her that men did bad things when they were drunk.

She'd just have to be quiet as she passed them. And hurry. She must hurry.

As she made her way down the narrow road, she could hear the laughter coming from some of the shacks. One man was singing at the top of his lungs, but they were all inside. Thank God.

But when she'd just passed the last house, her luck ran out. Suddenly the door flew open and out came three huge, burly men.

And they were all staring at Patience.

"Would you loo' at this, men!" one of them drunkenly exclaimed.

The one in the middle, whose hair was redder than any hair Patience had ever seen, walked toward her. "Are you looking for me, darlin'?" he growled.

Patience screamed and turned to run. But her feet failed her for the second time that night. She tripped over the hem of her dress and went sprawling in the dirt.

Suddenly they were all kneeling around her, pulling at her. "No, no. . . Please. . . Leave me alone! Please. . . ," she cried, as she tried to fight them off. *Oh, God, please, God. Don't let them hurt me. Please, help me, oh, God!* She prayed fervently.

Then God sent a miracle.

The click of the gun cocking was what stopped them,

but the voice was what sent them running. "Let her go and get back to your houses."

Patience looked at the owner of that hard, commanding voice and saw the uncompromising face of Bobby Joe Aaron.

"Oh, Bobby Joe. . . ," she wept. "Thank you. Thank you so much."

He knelt down beside her and gently helped her up. "What in the world are you doing out here, Patience? Don't you have more sense than this?"

She stood with his help and looked down at her soiled dress. Her hands were skinned and her hair was cascading all about her shoulders, having completely fallen from its knot. "My wagon broke down and I was trying to find you. I've been at Susannah Butler's house," she explained and looked up at him.

He opened his mouth to say something, but then stopped and stared at her.

She stared back warily. "What's the matter?"

Bobby Joe shook his head, bemused. "You. You look. . . different." He reached out as if to touch her hair but, at the last minute, caught himself and drew his hand back. His face, once again, became unreadable.

Patience just stared at him, not quite knowing how to take that comment. She'd known Bobby Joe all her life, though their families rarely socialized. And since he was almost ten years older than she was, Patience could count on one hand the number of times that she'd actually spoken to him.

His words seemed to hang awkwardly between them. "Well, let's get you back to the house. I'll send some men down to see about your wagon."

Patience nodded and wondered if the rest of the time in his company was going to be as strange as this had been.

ten

The Aaron house was massive. All three stories of it stood tall among the beautiful pines that surrounded the home. It was the only house in Springton that was made of brick. Jeremiah Aaron, Bobby Joe's great-grandfather, had hauled them in all the way from Chicago. There were three tiers of porches and balconies that were supported by six huge, white pillars.

It was the first time that Patience had ever been in the house. She was more than a little intimidated as she stepped over the threshold and onto the shiny marble floor.

Bobby Joe closed the door behind him and offered to take her shawl. She turned her back to him, and he took the garment and threw it and his own jacket over the hat tree standing by the door.

"Why don't we go into the library," Bobby Joe suggested as he gestured toward an open door off the hallway. "There should be a fire in there so you can warm yourself."

She nodded, but her mind raced. A library? People actually had libraries in their houses? Goodness!

Patience had never seen so many books in her life. Being a book lover, she yearned to pore over the titles to see what she could discover.

Instead, she followed Bobby Joe to the hearth, and together they held their hands out to the warmth of the crackling fire. She turned to thank him for his hospitality, but when she looked at him, she noticed that he was already looking at her. And probably had been looking at her the whole time.

Was there something on her face? Self-consciously she put a hand up to her cheek but felt nothing but her clean, chilled skin.

Why had he been staring? Her face must have reflected her confusion, because he suddenly blushed and quickly looked away.

Patience looked away also, more confused than ever.

"Well," Bobby Joe said after they stood there in an awkward silence. "I'll go tell my men to see about your wagon." And with a polite nod, he walked out of the room.

She opened her mouth to say something, but he was already gone. *Bobby Joe is a strange man*, she thought for the umpteenth time that night. With a shrug, Patience turned back to the shelves of worded treasures and smiled. She really hoped that he wouldn't rush. And without another thought for her rescuer, she grabbed a couple of books and began to read.

❧

Fortunately, they were able to fix the wagon wheel. Patience, her arms loaded with books that Bobby Joe had gallantly lent her, readied herself for her ride home.

She laid the books carefully in the back of the wagon, then turned to Bobby Joe, who was standing quietly by.

"Thank you, Mr. Aaron, for all your help." She paused and glanced toward the back of her wagon with a smile. "And for the books."

He actually smiled. Patience couldn't help but marvel

at what a handsome man he was when he allowed himself to relax. "It was nothing."

He looked down at his feet as he shuffled the toe of his boot in the dirt. "Look," he began, "I know it's none of my business, but a pretty girl like you don't need to be riding around unescorted. Next time, someone may not be there to rescue you."

Patience's mouth fell open in shock, and she stared at his nonchalant expression as he looked everywhere but at her. It was almost as if he was embarrassed saying it.

Then she realized something. Gruff old Bobby Joe Aaron was really a nice guy—he just didn't want anyone to know it!

And he thought she was *pretty*?

Blinking a couple of times in amazement, she looked away from him. "I'll be careful, Mr. Aaron. I don't ever want to be caught alone again. I thought they were going to. . ." Her voice faltered.

"But they didn't," he interjected firmly.

She nodded her head and looked at him. "Thanks to you."

He waved off her praise. "Here. Let me help you up."

He took her hand as she stepped into the wagon. Patience straightened her skirts, then picked up the reins.

Looking at him, she asked, "You'll be right behind me?"

He nodded and put his hat on. "I'll be behind you all the way. Don't worry."

She watched as he mounted his horse and realized that with him watching, she wouldn't need to worry.

❧

Patience's mother met her at the door and she didn't look happy.

"Where—have—you—been!" Prudence demanded, emphasizing each and every word. She was dressed in her plain, white nightgown that buttoned high on her throat. Her hair was still in its severe knot at the base of her neck. Patience thought fleetingly that she'd never once seen her mother with her hair down.

Patience looked away and brushed past her mother to step on into the room. "The wagon wheel broke," she said shortly. She was so emotionally drained, she didn't want to be having this discussion now.

Prudence closed the door behind her and stood, back stiff, with her arms folded tightly at her middle. "It didn't seem to be broken when you rode up!"

Patience took a deep breath and sank down into a chair. There was no way her mother would let her go easily; she would have to explain the whole thing. "I was coming home from Susannah's house, when my wheel broke. I was right by the Aaron brothers' sawmill when it happened. Mr. Aaron invited me in and then got some of his men to fix it for me, then he followed me home on his horse," she explained, deliberately leaving out the part of the attack.

Patience watched as a red, angry flush spread across her mother's face. "What if someone had seen you with that man? Don't you realize what would have happened to your reputation?"

Patience shoved her hair out of her face. "Mama, I didn't know what else to do, I—"

"I'll tell you what you don't do, Patience Anne—you don't go into a young man's home at this time of night! You should have waited outside!" Prudence raged.

"Mama, you don't understand the situation."

"Oh, I think I do understand! You just don't think, girl! Are you hoping that Bobby Joe Aaron will want to marry you, now? If you are, you are—"

"I was nearly raped!" Patience all but screamed at her mother. Tears of frustration pooled in her eyes. "I was trying to find the Aaron house when some of his men attacked me. If it wasn't for Mr. Aaron, I can only imagine what would have happened to me."

Prudence's face paled. "Patience, I. . ."

"He took me into the house to get me away from them and to make me feel safe. Which was the same reason he followed me home tonight. Because he was worried about me." Silent tears were flowing down her checks. Her eyes pled for her mother to understand, to offer her comfort.

Prudence stood up and walked to where her daughter sat. Her hand reached forward, and for a moment, Patience thought she was going to hug her. But then she pulled it back and stepped away. "Well, it seems you've had a rough night. You'd best get on to bed."

Patience watched her mother leave the room. A familiar sadness swept over her, urging more tears to fall. But she had cried enough. Determinedly she wiped her face with the back of her hand and stood to walk to her room.

She passed her small mirror that was perched on her dresser, then on impulse she stopped and looked into it.

Hesitantly, she reached up and touched the curls that surrounded her face. She'd always hated her curls; her mother had told her that they were unbecoming and she must wear her hair tightly knotted to hide them.

But Bobby Joe Aaron had remarked that she looked

different, even. . .pretty! No one had ever called her pretty before.

She sighed, pushing her hair away from her face in a frustrated gesture. "If only Lee thought I was pretty," she said aloud to her reflection.

But maybe with Rachel's help, he would.

❧

The next morning, before Patience left the house for her new job, a message was sent to them. "A message from the sheriff," Billy said as he handed the note to Patience.

For a day so full of promises, it was amazing how one little note could darken it so fast. Lee didn't want her to bring food around to him anymore. Said he was feeling well enough to eat at the inn once again.

The truth was, he did not want to see her anymore. He didn't want her bothering him. Especially after she made such a fool of herself last night. It was just as well, she thought, remembering her resolve to stay away from him. This would just make it easier to keep her promise to herself.

❧

The real truth was that Lee was having conflicting feelings about Patience, and it was getting in the way of his courtship of Susannah. He could not allow himself to see Patience anymore. He'd felt so terrible about laughing at her. She pulled at his emotions like no other woman ever had and he didn't want her to. She wasn't right for him. Susannah was the woman he needed.

He'd decided not to have her bring his lunches in an effort to push her away. He hoped she wouldn't be too hurt by his rejection.

He shook his head, trying to shake off his guilty feelings.

Today was a new day, he told himself. Besides, he had a date with Susannah to eat a picnic lunch and nothing was going to stand in his way.

Especially not Patience Primrose.

❧

By lunchtime, Patience knew she'd never worked so hard, but had so much fun. Adelaide Hayes was a tiny woman who had more energy than anyone Patience had ever encountered. Together they stacked canned goods, folded material, and restocked the dry-goods shelves.

Mrs. Hayes and her friend Maddie Mae Higgins were now dusting the books at the back of the store. Patience had offered her help, but the ladies insisted that they could do it by themselves. With a shrug, Patience donned her shawl and grabbed the basket of food that she'd packed for herself. Since it was such an unusually warm day, Addie had suggested that she take her lunch by the stream situated just behind the mercantile.

Humming softly to herself, Patience enjoyed the cool breeze blowing gently on her face as she walked. The water was surrounded by shade trees, but Patience decided to walk a little farther to find a nice place in the sun. It was still too cool for shade.

A small strand of hair came loose from her knot and blew across her face. Patience started to tuck it back, but stopped. Discreetly, she took a quick peek at her surroundings, then reached up and took the pins from her hair. Her scalp tingled as she shook her curly strands loose. She was prudent enough to pin the sides up. She didn't want to look like a ragamuffin!

She'd just walked around a clump of willow trees and when she saw what was on the other side, she froze.

To her dismay, there sitting on a beautiful blanket of blue and white lace was Susannah and sitting with her was. . .

Lee.

eleven

Turn around and pretend that you didn't see them! was the first thing that ran through Patience's mind. She didn't want to see this. She didn't want to see the man she loved cosying up to someone else.

But that idea blew away like feathers in the wind. For that very moment, Susannah looked up and saw her.

"Patience! Why isn't this just a pleasant surprise! Look yonder, Lee! It's Patience!" She tugged at Lee's arm. But he was already looking at her, though he didn't say anything.

Susannah apparently didn't notice his reaction because she hopped up and went to Patience. "And just look at your hair!" Susannah exclaimed, clasping her hands together in delight.

Patience reached up to her wind-tossed hair with a sinking feeling. She'd forgotten about her hair. Hurriedly she tried to explain. "I was just. . ."

"It's absolutely de–lightful! Patience Primrose, you stinker! You have the most beautiful hair I believe I've ever seen! Don't you agree, Lee?" she asked without looking at him for an answer.

That was a good thing, because when Patience glanced at Lee, he was still staring at her strangely. As a matter of fact, he was looking at her just like. . .Bobby Joe Aaron had the night before.

Susannah noticed Patience's picnic basket. "Were you going to eat by yourself?" she cried.

Patience nodded and opened her mouth to reply, but she wasn't given the chance.

"Why, we can't allow that, can we, Lee?" No response. "You must join us! Come, come! Sit! There's plenty of room for all three of us!"

Patience was horrified. "Oh no, I couldn't. I. . ."

Susannah sat down and started taking food out of her basket. "Oh, sure you can," she replied. "Tell her she can stay, Sheriff." This time the question demanded a response, and when she didn't get one, Susannah looked up at him. "Sheriff? Lee!"

Lee heard his name, but not all that clearly. Frankly, he'd been in somewhat of a stupor ever since he looked up and saw Patience standing there surrounded by all that. . .*hair!* Where had all those lovely curls come from? Suddenly a face that usually looked pale and plain and slightly pinched looked totally different when framed by her dark blond hair. She was. . .pretty!

She wasn't supposed to be pretty.

For some reason he didn't want to examine, he got really irritated. And he showed it.

"Why are you wearing your hair like that?" he snapped at her.

Patience looked away, her face losing its smile and becoming withdrawn. Beside him, Susannah gasped.

"Sheriff Cutler, sir! You're going to hurt her feelings! *Again*!" she added with emphasis. She cleared her throat and put a hand at her throat as if to collect herself. "Now, I think you owe Patience an apology so that she will feel comfortable joining us."

Lee grimaced at her tone. He could tell Susannah was a schoolteacher when she talked like that. It made him want to ask that she not send a note home to his mother!

And when had they invited Patience to join them? Wasn't this supposed to be a date? He specifically did not want to think about Patience, much less have her join them!

One look at Susannah's face changed his mind. She looked stern and disapproving. He wasn't sure he liked this side of her.

Reluctantly he looked at Patience, trying to squelch his feelings of concern over having hurt her again.

"I'm sorry, Patience," he told her, and he meant it. "You might as well join us. There's plenty of room."

❧

Well, when he puts it like that, how could I possibly refuse? she thought sarcastically. How could she not feel insulted at his treatment of her?

More and more, Patience was determined to set the man out of her mind. How could she ever think that this man was looking at her in an admiring way? He was probably thinking about something else when he'd worn that strange look earlier.

He was probably thinking of Susannah.

Maybe he didn't think she was pretty, but someone else did—Bobby Joe Aaron. Maybe she'd start casting her amorous aspirations *his* direction!

Who needed a man like Leander Cutler, who treated her so shabbily? Who needed a man who, for all accounts and purposes, was in love with someone else?

You do, her heart seemed to whisper to her. *You do. . .*

❧

The picnic was a disaster. Try as she might, Susannah could not generate a pleasant conversation or salvage whatever pleasant mood they might have started off with. Lee seemed uptight and uncommunicative the whole time, and Patience acted as if she might burst into tears if she talked too much.

Poor Susannah. Even she gave up after a while and joined them in their stilted silence.

❧

The picnic had turned a perfectly wonderful day into a dreadful one.

Patience was so upset about it, that she completely forgot that she was supposed to meet with Rachel after work.

She had just climbed up into her wagon when Rachel ran up to her. "Patience! Wait! Did you forget that you were supposed to come to my house?"

"Oh no!" Patience cried out in dismay. "I did, but let me tie the horses back up and I'll come right over."

Rachel smiled. "I'll wait for you and walk you over."

Patience smiled back, marveling at how she felt a kinship with this woman. One that, strangely enough, she was even feeling for Susannah. After a lifetime of having no real friends, two friends was a little overwhelming, but very welcome.

"All right," she called out and climbed from the wagon. At Rachel's house, Patience sat in a chair as Rachel slowly circled her, eyeing her closely. Her hand was on her chin with one finger tapping thoughtfully, while her eyes squinted with concentration. Patience heard a lot of "mmmm's" and "hmmm's."

"Okay, stand up," Rachel finally said.

She said it with such command that Patience immediately obeyed. Rachel might be little and petite, but she sure was bossy!

Rachel took Patience's measurements and worked with her hair for at least twenty minutes. She took her hair down and put it back up three different times in three different styles.

Finally, Rachel was satisfied with the way Patience's hair looked. She took a step back and smiled. "Perfect!"

Patience's eyebrows lifted with excitement. "Do you have a mirror? I want to see!"

"No."

Patience frowned. "What do you mean 'no'?"

Rachel held her arms out on either side of herself. "We're not finished. Now, follow me."

Patience sighed, but obeyed. She followed Rachel into her and Caleb's bedroom. She watched as Rachel went to her wardrobe and took out a garment made of peach-and-white cotton. The sleeves were puffed and edged with ruffles. The neck was rounded with a pretty white collar. The skirt was slim and slightly gathered with pleats at the back. It was so pretty and feminine.

"It's beautiful, Rachel!" she said wistfully.

"It's yours."

Patience looked at Rachel with disbelief. "It's mine?"

Rachel nodded. "I had made it for a lady in Tyler, but she decided on a different color. I held on to it, hoping I'd be able to use it for something else. After I talked to you last night, I came home and took some tucks and made a few adjustments. According to my measurements, it should fit perfectly." She held the dress out to Patience.

Reverently, Patience reached out and took the dress. Carefully, she held it with one hand, while touching the exquisite workmanship with the other. "I don't know how I can pay you, right now. I. . ."

Rachel laid a hand on Patience's arm. "It's a gift, Patience. You've been on my heart ever since Caleb and I returned from our honeymoon. I wanted to give you this so that when you wore it, you would know that someone was thinking about you and praying for you."

Rachel dropped her hand and smiled gently at Patience. "I've felt that you needed a friend, and I'll be honest with you—I've needed one, too."

Tears welled up in Patience's eyes. "I would love to have you for a friend, Rachel."

"Then, it's settled," Rachel declared, with tears in her own eyes. "Now, let's get that dress on so that you can see how pretty you look!"

Patience laughed. "I don't know about that, but I do want to get into that dress!"

After a lot of unbuttoning, buttoning, and straightening, the dress was finally on. Rachel stepped back, once again inspecting her work.

A look of pure wonder spread across her face. "Oh, Patience. . . ," she whispered in a voice filled with awe.

"What? Oh, Rachel, I want to see!" Patience cried impatiently.

Rachel took Patience by the hand and led her to a full-length oval mirror.

This can't be me was the first thing she thought upon seeing her reflection. The woman staring back at her was elegant and graceful. Patience Primrose was frumpy and plain.

Her hair was pulled up, but Rachel had cut strands of hair so that they curled and framed her face. And then there was the dress. In it, she didn't look like her too-skinny self, but rather slim and elegant. It fit her perfectly.

"I can't believe this is me." Her voice was full of wonder.

Rachel crossed her hand over her chest and looked quite pleased with herself. "Well, believe it!"

The sound of a door opening drew their attention from the reflection. Childish chatter and the clomp of little footsteps resounded throughout the house. Rachel's face lit up. "Caleb and the children are home! Come on. Let's show Caleb."

Suddenly, Patience was unsure of herself. "I don't think. . ."

Rachel rolled her eyes. "Come on, Patience. Courage, girl, courage!" Then she pulled her from the room and into the parlor where Caleb and the children were.

Caleb grabbed at his hat and took it off his head. "I didn't know you had company, Rachel." He held his hand out to Patience. "I'm Reverend Stone, ma'am. And you are?"

Patience looked at him in disbelief. "It's Patience Primrose, Brother Caleb. Don't you recognize me?"

Rachel playfully swatted his arm. "Caleb Stone, you are such a tease!"

She turned to Patience with a shake of her head. "Of course, he knows who you are, Patience. That's just his way of saying that you look nice."

She looked at Brother Caleb and saw the teasing glint in his eyes as he smiled at her. She wasn't sure what to say.

"I didn't mean to tease, Patience. I think you look very nice." He rubbed a finger across his chin as if contemplating something. "I cannot wait 'til Lee sees ya!"

Patience's mouth thinned. "Thank you, Brother Caleb, but I don't care if I ever see the sheriff again!"

The preacher winced. "Did I say the wrong thing?"

Rachel intervened. "Children, did you all have a good time looking at Harold Ray's new horses?" she said, addressing the children.

Jessie, the eldest of the children that they were in the process of adopting, answered, "Yes, ma'am. My favorite was the palomino!" he exclaimed, excited.

Emmy and Caitlin both asserted that they both liked the black mare with the white spot on its forehead.

Patience watched the family converse, grateful that the subject of Lee Cutler was dropped.

The reverend hit too close to the truth when he commented about Lee seeing her with her new look. She so wanted to know what he would think. She wanted to know if he thought that she looked pretty, that she could be someone he could love now that she looked different.

But her mind was made up. More and more she realized that if Lee didn't like her as plain Patience, she didn't want him. She wanted him to like her for her—not for what she looked like.

She once again looked at the reverend and his wife as they laughed with their children. Brother Caleb had loved Rachel despite what the town had thought of her. He wanted her for his wife, and nothing was going to get in his way.

That's the way Patience wanted to be loved. And more and more, she believed that God would help her find it.

Somewhere out there was a man who would love her and cherish her like the reverend loved Rachel.

She no longer believed it was the sheriff.

twelve

The next morning was Sunday, and everyone was sitting in their pews and listening to Brother Caleb introduce the soloist for that morning when Lee finally arrived. He couldn't believe he'd overslept. He had an old rooster that woke him up at 5:30 on the dot, every single morning. And Lee was sure that the ornery critter had probably crowed his heart out this morning, too, but he hadn't heard it. He'd slept right through it.

And it was all Patience's fault.

He couldn't believe it when she'd showed up yesterday at his picnic with Susannah. She must have planned it. Somehow she heard that he was taking Susannah on a picnic and she'd deliberately set out to sabotage it!

She wasn't going to get away with it. He was going to. . .

Just then, Susannah caught his eye. She gave him a little wave to let him know that she'd saved him a seat. Hurriedly, he made his way to the second row from the back and sat beside her.

He looked across the aisle and nodded to Billy and Daniel, then looked back to Susannah.

She smiled at him. As usual she looked pretty as a summer's day in her yellow dress made of silk. "I thought you weren't coming," she whispered close to his ear.

"I slept a little late this morning," he whispered back in response.

"You're just in time to hear her!"

He looked up to see who "*her*" was.

He should have known it'd be Patience. He dreamt about her, he saw her at dinner parties and on outings with other women, and she popped up in his mind at the most unusual times. Why should today be any different?

Only. . .wait a minute! This wasn't the Patience who sat by his bedside when he was sick, the one who laughed with him when he felt blue after being away from work so long. This wasn't the quiet, mousy girl who brought his meals and who ran away from a party after he'd cruelly laughed at her. No. This was someone different. Someone he didn't know! This Patience had her hair curled and styled and she was all gussied up in a shade of peach that made her skin glow like gold. A dress that fit her figure perfectly.

He hadn't known that Patience even *had* a figure.

What had she done to herself? First, it was the hair thing at the picnic and now this.

Lee didn't like this one bit. He had firmly convinced himself that he wasn't attracted to her and here she was making it harder for him.

Then she began to sing. It was not the first time he'd heard her, for she sang often. But it was the first time her voice affected him.

Her sweet, clear tones floated over him like a warm balm. He couldn't say what the song was, because all he could hear was the sincerity and passion behind those words.

He was captivated.

❧

Patience saw him come in and sit by Susannah. Not that

she cared, of course. It was merely an observation.

No, today was a new day. She was going to sing her song and step down. She wasn't going to look at the sheriff. Not once!

Okay. . .maybe one little peek. As she sang, she cast a quick glance his direction and then looked quickly away.

He was looking at her, and knowing that almost made her forget the words. Not wanting to take away from the meaning of the song by messing up, she firmly put Lee to the back of her mind, closed her eyes, and began to put her heart into it.

Patience loved to sing. She always thought it was the only thing that she did do well. It was the only thing her mother ever complimented her on, so she practiced often. And it was a way for her to forget her problems and dreary life. But best of all, she could express her feelings to God in a way she couldn't with a prayer.

When it was over, Brother Caleb came up and thanked her, and she stepped down to take her seat. Most of those who caught her eye were smiling at her with looks of appreciation, with a little wonder mixed in. They were obviously surprised at her new look.

And they weren't the only ones.

She hadn't meant to look at Lee, but her empty seat was situated right in front of him and Susannah. Her eyes just naturally went to him. For a moment, it seemed all time had stopped.

Their eyes met and held. Patience felt as though she couldn't look away. Something strange was happening to her, and it was wonderful and terrible all at the same time. Wonderful, because his warm gaze made her feel beautiful and wanted. Terrible, because she knew he was feeling something, too, yet he would continue to deny it 'til his dying breath.

And deny it he would. . .later. But not now. Not at this moment. Why couldn't he look away? Why did he feel as if he were drowning in her gaze? Emotions that he couldn't even begin to fathom were building up so heavily within his chest he felt as though he couldn't breath.

"Sit down, Patience! What's wrong with you?" Patience's mother hissed at her, yanking on Patience's skirt.

It made both of them jump, each becoming aware of their surroundings. Lee glanced around and to his chagrin everyone was staring at them! Even the preacher. In fact, Caleb was smiling at him as if he knew something Lee didn't.

As Patience whirled around and sat down, Lee felt his face burn and he knew that he must be the color of the Red River. He glanced over to Susannah, and she was giving him a searching look. He looked away, not wanting her to read what must have been clearly written on his face.

He was attracted to Patience Primrose.

He could deny it to his dying day, but there it was. It didn't mean anything, of course. He'd been attracted to a lot of women. This time was no different.

Just for reassurance, he reached over and took Susannah's hand. He heard her breath catch in a small gasp, and when he glanced at her, she was looking at him as though he were crazy.

Maybe he was crazy. Like a little boy that had just gotten his hand slapped for stealing from the cookie jar, he let go of her hand and placed it back on his own leg.

Things weren't going according to his plans. He was

supposed to be growing closer to her, building a relationship with her, not letting his foolish feelings for another woman get in the way!

Susannah was the woman he was going to marry. Now if he could just get her to believe that.

No. If he could just get himself to believe. . .

❧

Two weeks passed and no matter how hard Patience tried, she kept running into Lee. She knew that he thought that she was following him around, but she really wasn't. It was just that they were both working in town, and he always seemed to be going the same direction that she was going!

And worse, she always seemed to interrupt his attempts at courting Susannah.

If Lee wasn't irritated before, he was now.

Patience had done her best to keep him out of her mind. She worked three days a week at the mercantile and had earned the money to buy material, and Rachel was making her dresses out of it. She was wearing her hair in the style that Rachel had taught her, though her mother griped about it at every chance. But Patience was an adult now, and her mother just had to realize that!

Something else had happened to Patience that had never happened before. She began getting gentlemen callers! Men she'd never known existed were coming up to her and asking to escort her to church or were bringing her flowers.

She didn't know what to think. It was all very flattering, but she couldn't help wishing that they were the sheriff.

It was Saturday morning, near lunchtime. Patience had started to go up to Addie's room above the store to eat with her, when a knock sounded on their door.

Addie sighed. "I'd best go see who it is. It may be important."

Patience patted her on the arm. "You go on up, Miss Addie. I'll go check."

Addie nodded and went up the stairs.

Patience went to the door and was surprised to see Bobby Joe Aaron standing there.

"Oh! Hi, Mr. Aaron. Can I help you with something?" she asked, marveling at the way he looked. He'd really gone out of his way to fix himself up! His hair was all slicked back, and he was nicely dressed in a black vest and pants with a crisply ironed shirt.

Then she noticed the little girl standing beside him. It was his daughter Beth.

"Hi, Miss Primrose. Beth and I wanted to stop by to see if you'd join us for lunch," Bobby Joe asked her shyly. Shy was not a word one would usually apply to Bobby Joe, but he was sure acting timid!

Or was he just unsure of himself?

Patience looked at him, then looked down at his smiling daughter. "Oh. . .well. . .sure! Let me go and tell Addie, and I'll meet you back down here. All right?"

Bobby Joe nodded, and his daughter said, "Oh, goody. I told you she wouldn't say no, Daddy!"

His face turned red. "Beth, don't. . ."

"I'll be right back," Patience interrupted, not wanting him to take his embarrassment out on his daughter.

She did think it was funny, though. But she waited until she was out of earshot before she laughed aloud!

❧

Lee was sitting with Susannah in the dining room at the

Springton Inn. He'd asked her to lunch and felt pleased that she'd eagerly accepted. They were moving right along, now that he'd gotten his mind off of Patience. It was true that she kept popping up everywhere he went, but he was doing pretty well at staying focused on his courtship of Susannah. In fact, he was just about to invite her to attend church with him when *she* walked in.

"Not again," he groaned aloud without realizing it.

Susannah looked at him quizzically. "What's wrong?"

"Huh? Oh. . .nothing. I was just thinking about. . . something," he answered lamely.

She was something all right. Today, she was wearing blue. Not just regular blue, but rich, royal blue. The neckline was scooped and showed off a little of her chest and her neck. He noticed that her skin wasn't merely just pale, it was luminous.

"What is Bobby Joe doing with her?" Susannah whispered beside him.

What did Susannah mean? At that moment, he realized that Patience wasn't alone. She was with Bobby Joe Aaron and his daughter Beth! What was *he* doing with her!

But then again, why was Susannah worried about it? He glanced at her and saw a look of hurt cross her face, but it was quickly masked by a friendly, sunny smile.

He looked back and saw that the trio was headed their direction.

"Aunt Susannah!" Beth cried out and ran to throw her arms around her aunt. Susannah hugged her and greeted her with the same enthusiasm.

Slowly she looked up to her brother-in-law. "Hello, Bobby Joe."

Bobby Joe visibly stiffened beside her. "Hello, Susannah," he said coolly.

Lee frowned and wondered at the hostility that radiated between them. Then he wondered how Susannah could ignore Patience like that!

He had been ignoring Patience for two weeks now. He guessed it wouldn't hurt to be nice to spare her feelings today. He stood and greeted her. "Hello, Miss Patience."

Patience's face was an unreadable mask as she looked back at him. "Hello, Sheriff Cutler."

Lee's frown deepened. When had she stopped looking at him with adoration? Then it struck him that she didn't look like a woman who was pining away for him! Wasn't she affected at all after the way he'd ignored her?

And why was she with Bobby Joe Aaron? The thought kept menacing him.

"Can we eat with, y'all?" Beth asked. "Look! There's enough room!" She motioned to the three empty chairs at their large round table.

"Uh. . .I don't think. . .," Bobby Joe began.

"Well, we were just. . .," Lee chimed in.

"We really couldn't. . . ," Patience said graciously, causing the frown to return to Lee's face.

"Isn't that a wonderful idea!"

All eyes went to Susannah. She looked at everyone with innocent eyes. "Well, for goodness' sake! Are you all going to stare at me all day, or are you going to sit down and have some lunch?"

❧

It was a disaster. Maybe not as bad as the dinner party had been, but it was close.

Bobby Joe, who earlier had been friendly and a little

talkative—as much as Bobby Joe could be—suddenly clammed up and became a stone-faced grouch. Susannah was talking more than was even normal for her and trying to make everyone believe she was so happy, though it was obvious by the looks she kept sending Bobby Joe she wasn't.

And then there was Lee. He was acting just plain strange. He would look at Bobby Joe, then look at Patience, and a grim look would spread across his face. He did this about every five minutes, and after awhile, Patience got tired of it.

Leaving her plate barely touched, Patience pushed back from the table and stood. Immediately, the two men stood up with her. "I'd better get back to work." She turned to Bobby Joe. "Thank you for asking me to lunch, Bobby Joe and Beth. We must do it again sometime." *Alone*. She didn't say it, but it was clearly implied.

Bobby Joe nodded to her with an apology in his eyes. "Yes. We will," he agreed. "Can I walk you out?" He reached for his jacket.

She held out a hand. "No. That's okay. You sit and finish your meal." She smiled at Beth. "It was nice talking with you, Beth."

The seven-year-old waved at her.

Hurriedly, she said her good-byes to Susannah and Lee and quickly made her way from the inn.

❧

Lee didn't even think twice about it. He jumped up, threw down his napkin, and excused himself. "I'll be right back," he mumbled and ran out of the restaurant.

In three quick steps he had caught up with Patience.

Steering her into a nearby alley, he then turned her toward him. "What's going on between you and Bobby

Joe Aaron?" he demanded.

Patience blinked a couple of times. "Pardon me? I don't see that it's any of your concern, Sheriff Cutler!" she announced huffily.

His lips thinned. "See? You know me better than you know him, and you don't call *me* by my first name!"

"For your information, *Sheriff Cutler*, I've known Bobby Joe since I was a child. And besides, he asked me to call him by his first name!"

"And I see that you gave him the same privilege," he charged, pointing a wild finger in the direction of the inn.

"That's right, I did!"

"Well. . . ," he blustered, searching for words, aware that he was behaving like a lunatic. "I don't like it!"

She actually laughed at him. "Well, la-de-da! I don't care if you like it or not!"

"Well, maybe you won't care about *this,* either!" He grabbed her by the shoulders and kissed her.

thirteen

Touching her lips was like getting zapped by lightning! Stunned, he let her go and stumbled back a step. He watched as she brought a hand up to her face, her eyes full of amazement.

For a moment, they did nothing but stare at each other and try to catch their breath.

Why had he done that? He'd been courting Susannah for over two weeks now, and he'd done nothing but hold her hand! Now, here he was kissing the one woman he did not want to become involved with!

At that point, he lost all reason.

"I do hope that you don't think that kissing me means anything!"

Her mouth fell open with a gasp. "I didn't kiss you! You kissed me!"

He pointed his finger at her. "Well, you made me do it! And besides. . .*you* kissed me back!"

She grabbed his finger and shoved it out of the way. "I didn't make you do anything, Sheriff Cutler!" she taunted. "I think you have been *wanting* to kiss me! That's why you did it!"

He narrowed his eyes at her mean little smile. "That's just wishin' on your part, Miss Primrose! It will be a cold day in El Paso before that will happen! And I want you to stop following me around, too!"

"I haven't been *following* you around! How dare you. . ."

"Every time I'm on an outing with Susannah, you show up! Don't tell me it's a coincidence!"

"Okay! I won't tell you! I'll just let you wallow in your conceit!"

"Conceit, is it! Don't tell me you weren't hoping that I'd court you when you told Doc to bring me to your house. Well, it didn't work then, and it's not going to work now! I'm not going to court you, Patience. Not ever!"

Lee thought he saw her wince, but he wasn't sure. Even as the words were coming out of his mouth, he regretted what he said. But she rallied back quickly.

"Don't worry! I don't want you," she sneered. "Just make sure that you don't 'accidentally' kiss me anymore. I'd rather kiss. . .*Bobby Joe!* In fact, I just might do that. *Today!*"

His face darkened. "Now, don't you do anything stupid, Patience, I. . ."

"I didn't say you could use my first name, and I'll do whatever I please!" She started past him. "Now, if you'll excuse me. . ."

He grabbed her arm, but his grip was gentle. His face lost its anger, and a look of concern replaced it. "I mean it, Patience. Don't do anything stupid just to get back at me." He looked away for a moment, trying to collect his thoughts. "He's not a church-going man. You should keep that in mind."

She smiled at him sadly. "I'm not planning to marry him, Sheriff. And what do you care, anyway, huh? You've ignored me and. . .and laughed at me. . .and insulted me. You don't have the right to tell me anything." With that, she pulled her arm from his grip and walked away from him.

She waited until she was well away from him before she broke. She leaned against the backside of the store building and covered her face with trembling hands.

She was through with that man. She didn't want to see him and especially didn't want to talk to him. She wouldn't marry him if he was the absolute last man on earth!

Not that she ever would be given the chance.

❧

Patience showed up at church the next morning, sporting her new green dress. Rachel had told her it was the latest design from New York, and she had fashioned a small hat to match it.

While the dress caught everyone's eye, it was the little girl holding her hand that made everybody do a double take.

Patience could just imagine what they were all thinking of her coming in with Beth Aaron, but she didn't really care. The little girl was so eager to go, Patience couldn't have said no, even if she wanted to.

It was really the sheriff's words that made her bring up the idea with Bobby Joe in the first place. When he said that the sawmill owner wasn't a churchgoer, *Well* Patience thought, *it wouldn't hurt to invite him to go with me.*

Unfortunately, he turned her down, but Beth had chimed in that she would like to go. Bobby Joe didn't have any concerns about the matter, so they agreed that Patience and her mother would pick Beth up the next morning.

As usual, her mother balked, saying that she could

just imagine what people would think! Instead of riding in the wagon with her daughter, Prudence went with a neighbor.

That was fine with Patience. She didn't feel like dealing with her mother anyway.

She guided the little girl into the nearest pew, not really looking at whom she was sitting by. She got Beth all seated and patted her on the head. Then she looked up at the person just on the other side of the child.

She really should start paying more attention. . .

❧

Lee watched as Patience came in and sat by Susannah and himself. He noticed that she looked well rested and refreshed.

At least somebody *got some sleep last night.* He hadn't gotten any! He kept playing Patience's parting words over and over in his head, and he knew that he'd been behaving in a manner that was unbecoming and unchristian-like. Who was he to judge Bobby Joe, when he could treat another person the way he'd treated Patience?

He admitted to himself, finally, that he was very attracted to Patience Primrose. He didn't want to court Susannah, nice and pretty as she was. He wanted to court Patience.

He couldn't understand why it took him so long to figure that out. Probably it was because he'd been swayed by other's opinions.

Poor Patience was talked about and laughed about and called a plain old maid by every bachelor in town. He'd thought he was too good for her.

What a fool he was.

The truth was, Patience was too good for him. She was honest and kind, and someone with whom he could sit down and have a real conversation. She was a true friend and could be more than that to him.

But it could be too late.

He glanced down at the child beside her and wondered what was happening between her and Bobby Joe. Were they courting? He dearly hoped not.

Not when he wanted his chance at courting Patience.

"I can't believe it!"

Susannah's outraged whisper pulled his attention away from his thoughts of Patience. He looked sideways at her and saw that she was near to crying. "What's wrong?" he asked, his voice full of concern.

He watched as she looked over at Beth with a longing expression, then looked back to the preacher. "Nothing."

Huh? He sighed silently, and then glanced Patience's way. As if she felt his gaze, Patience turned her eyes to him. Then she lifted her head, looked down her nose at him, sniffed, then looked away.

Lee had just been royally snubbed!

Great! he thought morosely. He was sitting by two women who either hated him or wanted to cry all over him for no reason.

He felt a pull at his sleeve and he looked down to see Beth staring at him. She grinned, showing him two big spaces in her mouth where teeth should be, then she winked at him!

He bit his lip to keep from laughing, then he moved his eyes back to the preacher.

At least somebody liked him!

❧

She couldn't *believe* she had sat by Lee Cutler! Of course, he would think she did it on purpose, the conceited man!

Well, let him! She no longer cared what he thought.

Susannah could have him!

❧

Lee was taking Susannah back to his house, when he decided to ask her again what was wrong. She'd been strangely quiet ever since they'd left the church.

Susannah sniffed and blinked, obviously trying hard not to cry. "I've been asking Bobby Joe for months now to let me spend time with Beth. He always says no. Do you know that he won't even let her come to the town school? He hired a tutor to come to his house three times a week to teach her. It just hurt my feelings, I guess, to see that he allowed Patience to bring her to church." She looked off in the distance for a moment, then looked down at her clenched hands. "I guess they're getting close, huh?"

Her words struck fear into his heart. He wasn't the only one thinking it, then. "I don't know, Susannah. What's between you two anyway?"

She shook her head. "I don't know. I guess he blames me for my sister running off. Then to find out she died without him ever being able to understand why she did it. . ." She let out a breath. "She left for reasons that I don't understand and by the time she reached our parents' house, she was dying. There was nothing I could do. Nothing anyone could do."

"Well, he's a lot different since his wife died. He's really bitter."

"I know," Susannah answered sadly. "I just wish I

could help him." She shrugged her shoulders. "Maybe Patience can."

Lee felt like shouting No! He didn't want Patience helping anybody but him!

They were silent for a moment. Lee knew what he had to do, he just didn't know how or the right words to say. He took a deep breath and just told her.

"Susannah, there's something I need to tell you. . . ."

"You're in love with Patience," she interrupted him calmly.

"Now, I've never said anything about. . .about. . .*love!*" he sputtered. "I just. . ." He stopped suddenly and looked at her with amazement. "How did you know what I was going to talk about?"

Susannah smiled at him and patted him on the cheek with a gloved hand. "Oh, Lee. It's been obvious to me for weeks. I was just wondering when you were going to notice."

Lee scratched his head. "But I thought you'd be mad at me for courting you all these weeks. . . ."

"I'm not in love with you, either, Lee, so you can quit worrying."

Lee opened his mouth and then shut it. "You're not?" he finally asked.

She laughed. "No, but I have really enjoyed your friendship. Now, what you need to do is forget about me and start working on winning over Patience!"

Lee blew out a frustrated breath. "I don't think she'll let me. And you said it yourself, she may be leaning Bobby Joe's direction."

Susannah sat back in her seat and crossed her arms

around her middle. "I hope not," she murmured.

Lee studied her face and began to realize things he'd totally missed before—that Susannah had her own feelings for Bobby Joe. Why hadn't he seen it before? But he kept his thoughts to himself.

With a flick of his wrist, he snapped the reins to urge the team to a faster pace.

fourteen

It was two weeks later, and Patience was busy writing up Mrs. Perkins's purchases when Lee walked in the door.

She determinedly ignored him as he milled around the store. "Here you go, Mrs. Perkins. You have a nice day," she told the newly married woman while handing her the bundle of goods.

Mrs. Perkins left and Patience got out a dust rag and began to wipe down the counter.

Lee sauntered over to her and leaned against the edge of the counter. "Hello, Miss Patience," he greeted.

She made a show of cleaning a spot on the counter that was well away from him. "Sheriff Cutler," she greeted coolly.

He walked to where she was. "When are you going to stop ignoring me, Patience?" he said with simmering impatience.

She avoided looking at him and walked to the opposite end of the counter. "The last I heard it was still pretty warm in El Paso, Sheriff Cutler. And I *didn't* give you permission to use my Christian name!"

Lee shoved a hand into his hair and smoothed it back in a show of frustration. "Come on, Patience. It's been two weeks since I said that. When are you going to forgive me?"

She turned to him finally, looking down her nose at him. "You're forgiven. Now, if you'll excuse me, I've got work to do." With a regal lift of her chin, she went to an aisle where she had started stocking paper and pencils.

"Well, if you forgive me, will you go with me to the fall social the ladies club is throwing this Saturday?" he asked while following her.

She kneeled on the floor and took a stack of tablets out of a box. "No. I already have a date." She carefully placed them on the shelves and prayed her hands wouldn't shake.

She still had deep feelings for Lee, no matter how she tried to convince herself otherwise. But she knew he was only coming around and inviting her out because he felt guilty for saying all those mean things to her. He didn't really want to be with her.

"Who is it this time?" he stressed. "This is the second man who's called on you this week, and it's only Tuesday." She'd been called upon at her home by Jake Smith, Harold Ray's widowed son.

She smiled with satisfaction, knowing that her loose hair hid her face. "Not that it's any of your business, but I'm going with Bernard Touchet."

"The Frenchman?" he exclaimed with derisiveness.

"He's not from France, but from Lafayette, Louisiana. I suppose you could call him Cajun French."

"He's only lived here for a month! You don't know what kind of man he is." Lee was pacing back and forth at this point.

Patience started counting the pencils in the box. "And I suppose you do?"

Lee stopped and looked down at her blankly. "Well. . . No! And that's the reason you don't need to go to the social with him!"

Patience looked up at Lee curiously. He sure was acting funny. "I didn't realize your role of sheriff extended to who courted whom!"

Lee's mouth thinned. "Okay, here's another for you. The man is in his mid-forties! He could be your father!"

Patience sighed and threw the remaining pencils back in the box. She kept losing count. Unless she got rid of him, she was never going to get any work done. Slowly, she stood and dusted off her dark blue skirt.

"I am tired of having this conversation. Aren't you supposed to be guarding that outlaw or something?"

Lee shook his head absently. "I'm on night duty. Billy is with him now."

Patience planted her hands on her hips. "And I suppose you haven't been home to rest, either, have you?"

Lee shook his head. "No, but. . ."

She took the sheriff by the arm to pull him toward the door, but she had forgotten what touching him did to her. It made her go all soft inside. It made her dream of him taking her into his arms and kissing her again.

She was so moved by the warmth of his arm that she just stood there.

Lee felt it, too. Carefully, so as not to scare her away, he covered her hand with his own. The touch of her soft skin brought back memories of their kiss. How wonderful it felt having her in his arms.

He wanted more. He wanted Patience to be his wife.

But he couldn't just blurt something like that out. No. He had to woo her and court her.

That was, if she'd let him!

Patience had been more than stubborn for two weeks now. He knew that she still felt something for him. He also knew that he'd hurt her badly. It was going to take time to win back her trust.

And now that she'd been going out with other men, he knew that she wasn't getting serious about Bobby Joe Aaron, so he had more time to win her.

But what was with this Frenchman? He'd come into town last month and bought a large spread just outside of town. Already he was building a house that rivaled the Aaron mansion. That meant he was rich. How could Lee compete? Lee was a man of comfortable, but meager means. He couldn't give Patience a big fancy house or fancy clothes.

What he could give her was his love.

Love! He'd never thought about it much, but it was true. He was in love with Patience Primrose.

She was still holding onto his arm and looking at him. He was so overwhelmed by his feelings for her that he did what came natural.

He bent to kiss her.

Dingaling-aling-aling! The sound of the bell made her jerk away from him.

Lee tried to pull her back, but it was too late.

Startled, Patience looked at him with accusing eyes, then ran to the front of the store.

Though frustration gnawed at him, he took deep breaths and forced himself to be calm.

And he stayed that way until he saw who had come in the door.

It was the Frenchman.

Patience smiled at Mr. Touchet as he walked up to her. Lee had completely gotten the wrong idea about them, and she'd allowed him to believe it. In truth, she enjoyed

Mr. Touchet's conversations since he'd been coming into the mercantile, and she had felt a kinship with him, much like a niece with her favorite uncle.

He would tell her stories of his life in Louisiana and about their unique culture. And best of all, he'd seemed to enjoy talking to her, too. In fact, it seemed that he sometimes came to the store just to talk to her. He constantly wanted her to tell him about her life and the things that she'd done growing up. But most of all he made her feel good about herself. Something she hadn't felt in a long time, despite the wonders that Rachel had wrought in her appearance. While it was true, she was getting a lot of attention from the young bachelors in town, she couldn't forget Lee's words. She couldn't forget that he'd said that he'd never court her.

So she welcomed any chance she got to talk to the gentleman. Mr. Touchet was just a very nice, older man who probably thought she reminded him of his own daughter. Lee shouldn't have been so suspicious, anyway.

But he was. Lee didn't like the fact that this stranger was so chummy with the girl he was in love with. Who was he? What did he want?

Billy had reported to him that this Mr. Touchet came over to the mercantile quite a bit and only on the days that Patience worked.

Maybe he was one of those dirty old men who stalked helpless women! Well, he would just have to get through Leander Cutler first.

Bernard Touchet gave Lee a friendly smile. "Good evening, Sheriff!" he greeted in his accented voice. "How are you today?"

Lee nodded to the man without returning his smile.

"Howdy, Mr. Too-chet," he said in an exaggerated drawl, deliberately mispronouncing his name. "What brings you to town?"

"Oh, dis and dat," he answered vaguely. "I always drop in to say hello to de belle of all Texas!" he commented with exaggerated hand movements.

It was all Lee could do not to roll his eyes. The man was slick, he'd grant him that. One look at Patience and he could tell she was eating up all that malarkey he was shoveling out. It made Lee sick. . .

That he didn't think of it first.

Maybe that was why she was dating all those different guys. She liked all the attention. They probably flattered her and told her how pretty she looked.

He'd never once told her how much he liked her new look. Probably because he wished sometimes that she would go back to her old self so he wouldn't have so much competition.

And he wouldn't be so jealous.

"Well, you're right about that, Mr. Touchet," Lee finally answered, only he was looking at Patience. "She is the prettiest little lady around."

After making that comment he nodded to them both and left the store, pleased that he'd left Patience with her mouth hanging open in disbelief.

"De young sheriff, he's in love with you, yes?"

Patience managed to close her mouth and look at Mr. Touchet. "What did you say?"

Mr. Touchet waved in the direction of the front door. "Sheriff Cutler. He is in love with you," he confidently stated.

Patience just shook her head and laughed as if he'd told

a great joke. "Sheriff Cutler does not love me, Mr. Touchet. He feels bad because he hurt my feelings and he wants to make up for it. He's feeling guilty, not amorous!"

Mr. Touchet frowned. "Why do you not believe in yourself? You are a lovely and kind woman." He stared at her for a moment, then raised his eyebrows as if realizing something for the first time. "You do not think you're lovely or special, do you? You do not think dat a man such as de sheriff could love you!"

Patience looked away. "Mr. Touchet, I really have a lot of work to do and. . ."

He reached out and placed a hand on her shoulder. "You are, Patience. You are a special person. Do you not know dat all of God's creations are beautiful in deir own way? You must believe dat He made you beautiful, too. Not just on de outside, but on de inside!"

Bernard Touchet spoke with such conviction, she felt tears rising in her throat and eyes. If only she could feel that way. If only. . .

All she could do was shake her head.

Mr. Touchet nodded his head. "I see dat it will be up to me to see dat you believe! So just be prepared!"

That made her smile. "I will," she whispered through her tears. She wanted him to succeed.

But she wondered if he could.

fifteen

Patience sat in her kitchen, reading one of the books that Bobby Joe had sent her, trying to ignore the agitated movements of her mother as she furiously cleaned a room that was already spotless.

This particular behavior had been going on for a month now. Patience couldn't begin to understand what had upset Prudence, but she knew that something must have. When she'd asked, she'd been given some vague answer about there being nothing wrong.

But this was strange behavior for even *her* mother.

She thought about how Mr. Touchet had tried to help lift her spirits that very morning and wondered why she didn't try it with her mother. Prudence had never reached out to her, so Patience had never tried to reach out to her mother for fear of being rejected.

Well, Patience was tired of being fearful of doing things that might hurt her feelings. So she took a deep breath and began to talk.

"So, Mama, what did you do today?"

Prudence didn't miss a beat with her dusting. "This and that, Patience," she answered briskly.

Patience smiled in remembrance. "You know, I heard those very same words today at the mercantile. Only they were pronounced funny. But I guess they talk like that in South Louisiana. That's where Mr. Touchet is from, you know."

Patience didn't notice her mother had stopped dusting. "He's such a nice man. Have you met him yet, Mama? Mama?" she queried again when she got no answer the first time.

She stared at her mother's stiff back and frozen position. "Mama? Are you all right?"

Slowly Prudence turned, and Patience was shocked to see her mother's face was white. "You met. . .Mr. Touchet?" she asked faintly.

Patience nodded, not sure what was wrong.

Her mother was breathing fast and heavy. Prudence grabbed the back of the chair to steady herself. "Did he. . . say anything to you?"

Patience was getting scared. Her mother didn't look good at all. "What was he supposed to say, Mama?"

Her mother stared at her for a good long minute, then relaxed a little. "Nothing, I. . . Nothing," she muttered, shaking her head.

"Mama, do you know something about Mr. Touchet that I should know? He seems nice, but if he's a bad person, I need to know. I mean, he's escorting me to the fall social and. . ."

"He's what?" Prudence cried. "Oh, dear Lord. Oh, God. Help me. Please. . ." She grabbed at her chest and started the heavy breathing again. Then she stumbled backwards, almost falling.

Patience jumped up from her seat and ran to her mother. "Mama, what's wrong? Please. . .Talk to me!" She placed her arms around her mother's trim waist. She was shaking all over.

"This is terrible, so terrible. . . ." Prudence muttered over and over.

Patience was really scared now. Her mother was still clutching at her chest, and Patience worried that she could be having some kind of attack.

Slowly she led her mother to her bed and helped her lie down. Prudence seemed out of her head—she kept muttering things and now she was crying.

"What's wrong with you, Mama? Are you sick? Please tell me what I need to do," she begged her mother, but it was no use. It was as if she couldn't hear her.

There was only one thing to do. She had to go and get the doctor.

After closing her mother's door, Patience ran and grabbed her coat and put it over her nightgown, hurrying from the house.

There was no time to harness the horses, so Patience threw a saddle over one of them and prayed that she wouldn't kill herself riding into town. She'd never been any good at riding, but tonight she'd just have to take a chance.

For once, her mother needed her.

Clumsily she climbed onto the horse that she called Cactus, because she was always so prickly, and squirmed around until she got her seating. Cactus must have sensed her anxiousness, because for once she didn't try to throw her.

Wind whipped threw her loose hair and tore at her gown as she urged Cactus into a faster run than she was used to. It was so cold and her legs were partially exposed from straddling the horse. She forced herself to think about what she had to do to help her mother so that she wouldn't think about how badly her teeth were chattering.

Finally the dim glowing lamplights came into view. Doc's office was located in the middle of the town, just down the street from the sheriff's office. It was really a narrow two-story house that contained his office on the bottom floor and his residence on the top.

When she got there, she slid off her horse. Her leg muscles screamed in protest, and she almost stumbled. Determinedly, she made it to the door and pounded hard on the wooden surface.

"Doc! Doc, please wake up! It's Patience!" she yelled at the door. "Mother is ill! Doc! Doc?" It was no use. She could see that the lights were still out and the house was very quiet. With a sickening feeling, she realized that the Doc and his wife weren't home.

Frantically, she ran into the street and started searching for anyone who could help. Her eyes fell on the saloon. Raucous laughter filtered out into the night and made Patience shiver. It reminded her of the night she was attacked.

There was no way she was going *there* for help.

She looked down the other way and saw the sheriff's office. She let out a relieved sob when she saw a light burning in his window. Lee had night duty with the prisoner! He would know what to do.

She left her horse tied to Doc's post and ran to the sheriff's office.

❧

If he hadn't have been so exhausted, it wouldn't have happened. He'd tried so hard to stay awake, but the prisoner wasn't in the mood for chitchat, and he'd been unable to keep his eyes open. Somehow, he'd drifted off into a dreamless, exhausted sleep.

"*Click*!" was the only sound he heard, but it was enough. He went from very sleepy to wide-awake in a matter of seconds, which wasn't hard to do with a pistol pointed at his head.

Standing behind the gun was a face that only a mother could have loved. Black stringy hair fell from the man's pointed skinny head and around his stark face. He had sunken, beady eyes and a crooked nose. And when he smiled evilly at Lee, he displayed a mouthful of yellow, rotten teeth. It was a face he was familiar with. The outlaw's brother had returned for his own.

"Welllll, looky here!" he drawled snidely in his ready voice. "Looks like the law ain't too fierce around these here parts!"

The outlaw looked over to his brother. "Bubba, you all right?" he yelled out, looking quickly back to Lee.

"Yeah, but it sure took you long enough to get here," he whined.

Otis smiled. "Ain't that gratitude for ya?" he spoke to Lee. "He always was the spoilt one in the family." He laughed and Lee nearly doubled over from the smell of his breath.

Lee didn't say a word. He kept trying to think of a way to reach for his gun.

Otis finally stopped laughing at his own humor and got down to the business at hand. "Okay, Sheriff. Where do you keep those keys?"

Lee didn't say anything for a moment, but when he saw the deadness in the man's eyes, he realized that the man would as soon shoot at him as look at him. And Lee wanted to live. He wanted a life with Patience. He wasn't ready to die now.

"In the desk drawer," he replied coldly.

Otis moved in closer. "Well, why don't you get it?" he demanded, his voice sarcastic. "And don't try anything, because I'll plug you full of holes if you do!"

Sweat began to bead on Lee's forehead and fall down into his eyes. Slowly he reached down and grasped the drawer handle, pulling it open.

Lee looked at the keys, and then up at Otis. There was a gun inside the drawer. Did he dare?

His chance came when he saw Otis turn to his brother and say something. He got a good grip on the handle and trigger and started to lift the gun out of the drawer when the door opened.

Lightning fast, Otis whirled around and fired.

Everything happened in slow motion after that. The force of the bullet knocked Patience against the doorframe. Lee, shocked and horrified, reacted by aiming and shooting Otis. Almost in harmony, they fell to the floor.

Thinking his aim had been true, Lee dropped his hand and ran to where Patience lay. "Patience!" he cried, as he stepped over Otis to get to her.

Suddenly Lee was falling. Someone had grabbed his ankle. He managed to turn, as to not fall on top of Patience. He was just about to regroup and point his gun at the source of who made him fall, but he was too late.

Otis was already standing up, his pistol aimed steadily at Lee. Otis glanced at his bloody arm and laughed nastily. "You just nicked me, Lawman. I guess good help is hard to find in backwater towns like this, huh?"

Lee dropped his gun, his concern for Patience only. "Otis, listen. You have to let me check the girl. She's just an innocent bystander in all this," Lee pleaded.

Otis sneered as he picked up Lee's gun. "You can check her after I get Bubba out of here."

Slowly, he made his way to the desk and felt around for the key, his eyes and gun remaining on Lee.

Lee looked over to Patience. He could see the hole in her leather coat and the red stain on her gown where the coat gaped. But hope arose in his heart when he saw the faint movement of gown. She was alive!

He briefly closed his eyes and gave a prayer of thanks to God, then he opened them and watched as Otis let his brother out of the cell.

Then Otis waved his pistol in a gesture telling Lee to move into the cell. "Now it's your turn to spend a little time behind bars," Otis said with a terrible smile. "Pick the woman up and get in."

Lee cast a worried glance toward Patience and then looked pleadingly back at Otis. "Otis, please. She needs a doctor. If you'll just let me. . ."

"My heart's bleedin', Sheriff. Now quit wasting my time and get in here!" he ordered menacingly.

With a sinking heart, Lee lovingly gathered Patience in his arms and carried her into the cell. While he laid her on the cot, he heard the clang of metal hitting metal as the cell door shut. He didn't relax until he heard them leave the office.

Quickly, Lee stripped the coat off of her and ripped the gown open at the shoulder.

Tears of relief and joy gathered in his eyes when he saw the wound. It seemed that he hadn't been the only bad shot that night. The bullet had merely grazed her shoulder, and although it had bled a lot at first, it had already started slowing.

Patience hadn't fallen unconscious because of her wound. She had only fainted!

sixteen

"Patience. *Patience!*" She heard someone call from a long way off. What was touching her face? It felt like someone was tapping her cheeks. It certainly was annoying!

"Come on, Patience! Wake up!" *Tap, tap, tap. . .*

Well, the voice sounded like Lee, but Lee couldn't be trying to wake her up! Maybe her mother had a cold.

Tap, tap, tap. . .

Irritated, Patience slapped the object that was tapping her face. "Mmmm. . . Quit it," she mumbled.

She barely opened her eyes and saw Lee's face looming before her. "Oh. . .it *is* you," she said and then closed her eyes.

Two seconds later, her eyes sprang wide open as she stared at Lee in disbelief.

"Lee! What are you doing in my bedroom?"

Lee looked at her as though she'd lost her mind. "Patience, we aren't in your bedroom. We're at my office," he explained patiently. His face looked haggard and weary.

She frowned. "What are we doing in your office?"

He looked at her, biting his lip as if contemplating what to tell her. "Uh. . . You don't remember coming in here?" She shook her head, and he sighed. "Well, you did, and. . . you were shot." He pointed to her bandaged shoulder.

Patience looked over and saw the blood all over her nightgown. Then she noticed the bulk of the bandage that he'd made from a pillowcase underneath.

"You shot me?" she asked with disbelief. "Am I all right? I'm not dying, am I?"

Lee let out an aggravated breath of air. "No, I didn't shoot you, Patience! How could you think that? And you're not dying. Believe me, you wouldn't be this chatty if you were. You were just nicked; you're fine."

She shook her head and winced at the pain—her shoulder was really aching. "Who shot me, then?"

"Take it easy," he soothed, laying a gentle hand on the bandage, making sure it was still tight. "Remember the outlaw I was guarding?" She nodded. "Well, his brother caught me off guard and you got caught in the middle. Then they locked us up in here," he said, motioning about the cell.

She looked over at the bars. "We're in the jail cell!"

"Yeah. And I don't think we're going to get out of here until daybreak, when Billy comes in to relieve me."

For some reason the meaning of that comment didn't register because suddenly her memory was triggered.

"Oh no!" she cried, sitting up. She tried to ignore the pain in her shoulder. "My mother!"

"For goodness' sake, Patience! You're going to make it start bleeding again!" He checked her bandage again. "Now, what's this about your mother?"

She grabbed Lee's arm. "Lee, I think my mother is ill. I tried to find the doctor, but he wasn't home! That's why, when I saw your lights, I came over here!"

"I was wondering what you were doing out this late. . . especially after what happened to you the last time."

Her eyes widened. "You know about that?"

He nodded grimly.

She looked at him for a moment, then shook her head.

"Lee, we have to get out of here!" She jumped up, walking to the door and shaking it.

Lee followed her and took her by her good arm. "Patience, just calm down. We ain't goin' nowhere! Now tell me exactly what happened with your mother."

Patience reluctantly allowed Lee to lead her to the cot. "We were talking about me meeting with Mr. Touchet and she suddenly turned pale and began shaking like she couldn't stop. She grabbed at her chest and ran to her room." She looked pleadingly at Lee. "Sheriff, we've got to help her!"

Lee held his hands up, trying to calm her down. "Whoa, there. Now it seems to me that your mother wasn't ill, she was just upset over this. . .this Touchet feller." He snorted. "She ain't the only one!"

Patience frowned. "But why would his name upset her? She's never met him."

Lee was thoughtful for a minute. "But what if she had? What if he did something to scare her and she is afraid. Has she been acting differently since he came into town?"

Patience thought back over the last month and how her mother rarely left the house. "Now that you mention it. . . she has been acting strange," she admitted.

"Okay, now think about this. She knows something bad about him and is scared of meeting up with him, then you come along and say that you are acquainted with him, and she gets upset!" Lee surmised.

She didn't look convinced. "I don't know, Sheriff. What if you're wrong? What if she's really sick?"

Lee sighed and leaned against the wall. "Then worrying about it ain't going to help matters none. We just have to pray and hope for the best."

Patience looked at Lee and felt strength and comfort radiating from him. He made her feel so secure when she would have otherwise felt so bad. "Sheriff? Will. . .you pray with me?" she asked timidly.

He smiled and held out his hand to her. "Sure, just take my hand."

She laid her hand in his large callused one and bowed her head.

Lee felt the familiar jolt that he usually felt when he touched her. This time it was coupled with something else—he felt fiercely protective of her. He wanted to take her fears away and be her strength. But all he could do was pray.

But it was enough.

"Dear Lord, we first thank You for keeping us safe from death or serious injury. We know that it could have been worse. But, Lord, we want to ask You, now, to look after Patience's mama. If she's ill, we ask that You heal her and if she's upset, we ask that You comfort her. We thank You for hearing and answering our prayers, Lord. In Your name, Amen."

They lifted their eyes and stared at each other. Lee wanted to say something to her, to make it all right, but he couldn't think of a word to say.

The silence became awkward, and Patience looked away with a blush staining her cheeks.

Lee let go of her hand. He stood up from where he'd been kneeling by the bed and began to pace the cell.

So many words popped into his head. So many things he wanted to tell her. Did he dare? Of course not. Now was not the time to announce that he was in love with her! She would probably think he was crazy!

So he decided to ask the question that had been burning in his mind for weeks now. "Are you and Bobby Joe still courting?"

She looked at him with a blank expression on her face. "Bobby Joe? I was never being courted by Bobby Joe!" she said with a slight laugh.

Lee was confused. "But I kept seeing you with him all over town, and then you brought his daughter to church."

Patience rolled her eyes. "Oh, for goodness' sake! I was just trying to talk him into letting Beth attend church and school. He is so unsure on how he should raise her, so I thought that I would help him."

Lee stared at her and thought of all the sleepless nights he worried that they were getting serious!

Patience tucked her hair behind her ears and then smoothed the covers at her waist. "So," she began in a conversational tone, "what about you and Susannah? Have you proposed yet?"

He looked at her and then looked away, hiding his smile. She knew good and well that he and Susannah did not see each other anymore. But he answered her anyway. "No. We've decided that we're not suited."

"Oh," was all she said as she went back to smoothing her covers. "I suppose that's good, then. I mean. . .that you've realized you're not suited before you get married."

Lee continued to smile. "Yes, it is. . . ." He wiped the silly grin off his face and turned to where she was. "Well, I guess we better get to sleep. I'll just take the extra blanket and bunk down over here," he told her, pointing to the other side of the cell from where she lay in the cot.

Wearily she nodded and scooted down in her covers to lie flat.

He walked over to her. "Does your shoulder hurt?" he asked with concern as he checked her bandage again.

She shook her head. "Not really. I just feel dirty with all this blood caked to my skin and clothes."

Lee smiled and reached for the blanket. "Tomorrow will come soon enough. Just get some sleep."

"Goodnight, Lee," she called out to him when he'd rolled himself up in the blanket on the hard floor. Her voice sounded sleepy.

Lee smiled when he heard her using his first name. "Goodnight, darlin'," he said on impulse and waited for what she'd say.

But from the other side of the room came nothing but silence.

❧

Sighing, Lee tightened the covers around himself and tried to think of anything that would take his mind off of how cold and hard the floor was.

But most of all, he didn't want to think about how close Patience was and the fact that he still could not call her his own.

"Oh, Dear Lord in Heaven, spare us all from the shame!"

The sound of Prudence Primrose's screechy cry brought both Patience and Lee fully awake. Like a shot, they bolted up in sitting positions from their make-shift beds.

Patience, still covered with the blanket, grabbed her shoulder and winced. Lee clutched at his back and did the same. It had not been a restful night for either of them.

"This is disgraceful!" her mother announced.

Patience blinked a couple of times and then smiled. "Mama! You're all right!" she cried joyfully.

Prudence's mouth drew up tightly as if she'd been sucking on a lemon. "I most certainly am *not* all right! I cannot believe it has come to this." She sniffed. "Well, I must do the only thing I can and do it quickly before the scandal spreads!"

After that little speech, she whirled around and marched out of the room, leaving a bewildered Patience looking after her.

She looked over at Lee and saw him gripping the sides of his head. "What did she mean?" she wondered aloud.

He shook his head. "I don't know, I wasn't listening. Have you ever tried sleeping on a floor? My back hurts, my head hurts, and I feel like I'm getting a cold or something," he complained.

Patience looked at the man and then rolled her eyes. Good grief! What a complainer! With a sigh she lay back on the cot. "She left without letting us out!"

Lee finally focused on Patience. "Why did she do that?"

"I don't know. She said something about a scandal and walked out!"

There was silence from Lee's side of the room for a moment, before Patience heard him say, "Uh oh."

Before Patience could say another word, the door to the office opened. Patience sat back up and looked at the door and then looked at Lee with question. But he wasn't looking at her—he was staring grimly at the people who had just walked into the office. They walked until they stood in front of the cell door.

Her mother was back. But she'd brought someone with her.

Reverend Caleb Stone.

"Well," Brother Caleb began. "Let me be the first to congratulate you both."

Patience frowned. "For what?" She looked again at Lee and wondered why he was being so quiet.

"Why, on your marriage, of course!"

seventeen

"My *what?*" Patience asked, aghast.

Brother Caleb opened his mouth to reply, but Prudence beat him to it.

"What are you doing in here with the sheriff, young lady? Don't you realize the shame. . .the disgrace, *humiliation*. . .the. . .the scandal, the. . ."

Brother Caleb interrupted her. "Mrs. Primrose, I think you better let me explain to them why you think they need to marry."

"There's no time for explaining. Just get on with the ceremony!" Prudence demanded, folding her arms tightly across her chest.

"Wait!" Patience cried. "You don't understand." She looked at Lee. "Well, say something, Lee!"

He looked at her calmly and shrugged. "What do you want me to say?"

She couldn't believe he was being so calm about all this! "Tell them what happened. About the outlaws and . . .and the shooting!" She pulled the blanket down exposing her bloody gown. "I was even *shot!*"

Brother Caleb looked incredulously at Lee. "You shot her?"

Lee scowled. "No, I did not shoot her. Why does everyone naturally assume it was me?"

"Patience Anne Primrose!" her mother screeched. "What are you doing in your nightgown?" She put her hand on her forehead. "This is worse than I thought."

Patience couldn't help but be hurt that her mother was not concerned about her being shot or locked in the jail cell by outlaws.

"Lee, is Patience all right? Who did this?" Brother Caleb interjected.

"Oh, the scandal of it all. . ."

"It was the prisoner and his brother."

"How could you leave the house wearing only your nightgown?"

"You mean they escaped?"

Patience closed her eyes, her head was spinning with everything that had happened to her and what was going on now. Everything was so chaotic. So mixed up. So confusing!

"*Stop it!*" she yelled out to the room as loud as she could. She opened her eyes to find all three of them staring at her as if she were crazy.

But at least they were quiet.

"I want everyone to be quiet and listen for a moment, okay?" She looked around the room and glared at them all until they nodded in agreement. Quickly, she told them everything that had happened, from her trying to find the doctor, to how they ended up in the jail.

There was nothing but silence that followed her incredible story.

Prudence cleared her throat. "Well, be that as it may, it doesn't matter. You did spend the night together, all alone, therefore, you must get married."

"No!"

"Okay."

The words were spoken at the same time.

"I cannot believe you agree to this!" Patience looked at Lee.

Lee just shrugged. "It doesn't look like we have much choice!"

Patience knew that was the way he felt—that he was only agreeing to the marriage because her mother was forcing him. Because of appearance. It just stung to hear it from his lips. She lowered her eyes and looked away.

As soon as the words were out of his mouth, he wanted to take them back. That wasn't what he wanted to say at all! He wanted to tell her that he wanted to marry her because he loved her! But thanks to his big mouth, she'd never believe it now.

"Patience. . .I. . ."

"What do you mean, *no*, young lady!" her mother demanded.

A defiant, determined look came over Patience's expression as she faced her mother. "It means that I will not marry Leander Cutler! It's humiliating to marry a man who feels forced into it!"

"Patience, that's not. . ."

"Miss Patience, I realize that it's not the most ideal way to get married, but I was under the impression that you and Lee were friends. Surely a marriage based on friendship can grow into love," the preacher tried to council.

Lee tried again. "But I already. . ."

"That wasn't the way you felt about Rachel, was it, Brother Caleb? You both already loved each other. That's what I want!" Patience told him with quiet conviction.

"But I can. . ."

Once again Lee was interrupted and he felt so frustrated he didn't know what to do!

"Oh, for goodness' sake, get on with it, Reverend!" Prudence ordered, her impatience evident. "And you, Patience! Not another word!"

"I won't do it!"

"You must do it!"

"Patience, I. . ." Lee tried to butt in.

"Patience, please be reasonable—"

"I am being reasonable—"

"I'm trying to tell you—" Lee tried again.

"You have to marry him."

"I don't."

"I am trying to say something here!" Lee yelled out over their voices. Once they were silent, he continued, "Now that I have your attention, I would like to tell Patience something."

He turned to her and looked into her eyes. "Patience, what I've been trying to tell you is that I. . ."

"What's going on in here?" a new voice interrupted Lee.

Everyone turned to see that Bernard Touchet had walked into the office, and he didn't look happy.

Lee's shoulders drooped. Why was this so difficult? He just wanted to tell her he loved her!

"It's none of your business! Now, please leave!" Patience's mother told the Frenchman coldly.

Lee, Patience, and Caleb were all shocked at her frosty tone. She sounded almost hostile!

Mr. Touchet's face turned an angry red. "It is so my business! Why is Patience locked behind bars? And why is she covered with blood?"

The preacher tried to soothe the strange situation. "Uh,

Mr. Touchet, sir, we are having a private conversation here. I'm sure that we can talk to you later."

Mr. Touchet ignored the preacher, his eyes staying steadily on Prudence. "You know that I have a right to know."

If steam could come out of Prudence's ears, Lee was sure that it would be doing it at that very moment. "You gave up that right a long time ago. Now, leave!"

Patience jumped up from the cot and walked to the cell door. "What does that mean, Mama? How do you know Mr. Touchet?" Patience asked in a strangely frightened voice.

Lee's protective instincts rose up within him and he quickly went to stand behind Patience. "Could you please let us out and then we can continue this conversation after Patience has been checked out with the doctor?"

Caleb shook his head. "But we don't have the key!"

Lee sighed and wondered what else could possibly go wrong.

"Should you tell her or shall I?" Bernard Touchet asked Prudence. Apparently they were in their own little world over there. They hadn't stopped glaring at each other once!

"Tell me what?"

"No one is telling her anything!" Prudence told him.

"That I'm your. . ."

"Goodness! What's all the hoola-ba-hoo? Did someone have a party and forget to invite me?"

Lee groaned inwardly and decided that it *could* get worse.

Susannah sashayed into the room and came up to the jail cell. "Oh, my stars! What are you two doing in there?

And, Patience! You're bleeding! What happened to you? Is everyone going to just stand there or are you going to let them out?" she demanded to the room at large.

"We don't have the key," the preacher started to explain.

"I was shot, Susannah!" Patience told her friend.

"Lee shot you?"

"No, I did not. . . ." He stopped and threw up his hands and stalked away from the cell door. "Forget it, just forget it!"

He turned back to them. "Can somebody go and find Billy? He's got an extra key."

"Reverend, can you please just marry them before the rest of the town finds out?" Prudence cried out desperately.

"Marry? Are you and Lee getting married?" Susannah asked.

"No!" Patience answered emphatically. "But they are trying to make him marry me!"

"They are not making me do anything. I. . ."

"But this is wonderful!" Susannah cooed.

Patience just shook her head in confusion. "Why is it wonderful?"

"Could somebody please go and get Billy?"

"I'm right here!" Billy announced from the doorway.

Lee let out a breath of relief. "Please tell me you brought the key to the cell door."

"Don't let them out before you pronounce them man and wife!" Prudence demanded.

The preacher shook his head. "But, Mrs. Primrose, I can't do that until they say their vows and. . ."

"And I'm not going to say them!" Patience announced. "Billy, open this door now!"

Billy fumbled in his pocket for the key and when he

brought them out, they were immediately snatched out of his hands.

"They are not coming out until they are married!" Prudence declared, holding the keys in the air where they were promptly snatched from her own hands.

"If she doesn't want to marry, she doesn't have to!" Bernard Touchet declared, now holding the keys in his hand. He stepped closer to the lock.

Prudence threw herself in front of it. "I will not let you do this! You don't belong here!"

"I do belong here, Prudence. Now, move!"

"Excuse me!" Susannah's Southern voice broke into the chaos. "I know it's none of my business, but I'm awfully curious. Why do you think you belong here, Mr. Touchet? Are you wanting Patience for yourself?"

Mr. Touchet sputtered, "Of course not! Do not be so ridiculous!"

Lee knew that this was not the time to go into this, but he'd been wondering the same thing about the Frenchman. He walked back to the cell door and looked right into the eyes of Touchet. "Then, why don't you tell us why you're here."

Bernard Touchet looked at Prudence. "Tell them," he ordered her.

"No," was her answer.

His mouth tightened grimly, and he looked at Lee, then past him to Patience.

For some reason, Lee reached out and put his arm around Patience, sensing she would need his comfort.

And he was right.

"I'm your father, *chére*."

eighteen

Lee was the one who took Patience to the doctor's office after Mr. Touchet finally let them out. Patience hadn't said a word since her father had shared his secret with everyone, and Lee was worried about her.

She had gone so still and pale, only looking at her mother in question. But Prudence wouldn't make eye contact with her. Silently, Lee had taken her arm and led her out of the jail and out of the building.

Now Lee was pacing around in Doc's outer room because Doc insisted that he couldn't come in while he examined her.

Lee looked despairingly at the closed door and wondered what was happening. Was Patience all right? What would this revelation mean to their future? Would it make a difference?

Not that it mattered to him. He loved Patience no matter whether she was born legitimately or not. But he could not predict what Patience would do. She'd been so adamant about not getting married before, he feared this would just give her another excuse to refuse.

What would he do without her?

Lord, please help us find a way through all this mess! And please let Patience realize I'm telling her the truth when I tell her that I love her. . . .

"You can come in now," Doc said as he peered around the door, interrupting Lee's prayer.

Quickly, Lee followed Doc into the room and found Patience sitting on the examination table, robed in a large brown dress. It obviously belonged to Doc's wife, but Lee was happy to see her out of the bloody nightgown.

He walked up to her and reached for her hands that lay folded in her lap. "Patience, darlin'? Are you all right?"

He was relieved when she looked at him tiredly and gave him a half smile. "I'm okay." She looked down at their entwined hands and when she raised her gaze back to his, she had tears in her eyes. "Lee, what am I going to do?"

Lee threw Doc a glance, and the doctor mumbled something about having to check on his wife, and then left the room.

Then Lee did what he'd been wanting to do ever since Patience had walked into his office last night. He put his arms around her and held her.

She began to cry. The sound of it tore his heart right in two.

❧

She didn't mean to cry. But the moment that Lee put his arms around her, she couldn't help herself. Never in her whole life had anyone offered to hold her when she was hurting. And now this man, the man that she loved with all her heart, was offering her the very thing she'd needed so many times in her life.

Tenderness and compassion.

When her tears began to subside, he handed her his hanky to wipe her eyes.

"How can I ever forgive my mama?" she said in a ravished voice.

He gently took the hanky from her trembling hands

and began to wipe the places that she had missed. "Why don't you hear her side of things before you start worryin' about that."

"But she lied to me, Lee. All these years she's let me believe that my father was dead! And now I find out that not only was my father alive—Mama was never married to him!"

"Patience. . ."

"No!" she said firmly, pushing away from him. Her tears were gone, and anger had taken its place. "Do you know how judgmental she has been toward me all my life? She's never been considerate or kind to me. She's never taken me in her arms like you just did and offered me comfort. All she's ever done is rule my life!"

"Patience, I want you to calm down and listen to me," he ordered as he took her shoulders in his hands. She obeyed mainly because she was stunned that he'd used such a harsh tone with her. "I didn't mean to yell at you, but I need you to listen to me."

Just hearing his voice calmed her down. With him, she felt safe, as if she could lean on him and he'd take her problems on his capable shoulders. She nodded her head to him.

He took a breath and began to speak. "I think it's important to talk to your mother and I'll tell you why. Just think how she felt when she found out she was with child and unmarried. And why didn't Touchet do the honorable thing and marry her? It seems like the blame should not fall only on your mother's shoulders."

She opened her mouth to speak, but he stopped her. "No, wait. You said your mother was always strict with you and judgmental. Don't you think that she was just trying, in her own way, to make sure that you didn't make her mistakes? Yes, she went about it the wrong way. But in her mind, I'd imagine she did the best that she knew how."

Patience bit her lip and thought about what Lee was saying. "I know there is some truth in what you are saying but. . .I just don't know. . . ."

"I know that it won't be easy. Forgiving and forgetting will take time. But I know that God will help you if you'll just trust in Him." He took her hands into his once again. "I'll be here, too."

Patience looked into his eyes, afraid to read anything into that statement. "You will?" she asked faintly.

"Yes, I will, if you'll let me. Patience, I want you to marry me."

She felt as if she couldn't breathe. "You do?"

He smiled tenderly. "Yes, I do."

Patience wanted to believe that he wanted to marry her, but she told herself that it couldn't be true. Someone like Lee Cutler wouldn't want to marry someone like her. "You're just afraid of a scandal, Lee. You don't really want to marry me."

He actually laughed! "Oh, Patience, how can you even think that I would marry you for that reason! I'm not afraid of a scandal." He stepped back and tugged at her arms until she had scooted off the table and was standing in front of him. He let go of one of her hands and gently cupped her face in his palm.

"I love you, Patience. That's the reason I want to marry you."

Patience searched his eyes and face, looking for some sign that he wasn't telling the truth. But for the first time, she saw the love shining through his eyes and smile. "Oh, my goodness! You're telling the truth," she said faintly.

He nodded. "I'm telling the truth. Now, you tell me the truth. Do you love me?"

Patience wondered if the man was blind or just crazy! "Of course, I love you!" she cried. And with a jubilant laugh, she launched herself into his arms.

He caught her and hugged her tightly to him. "Ah, darlin', you've made me a happy man," he told her, then bent his head to kiss her.

After a moment, he looked up and asked her, "Does this mean you'll marry me?"

She nodded. "Yes! Oh yes, I'll marry you!" This time it was she who kissed him!

❧

Lee felt like a thirsty man that had finally reached the river. He returned her kiss, telling her without words the feelings that were swirling around in his heart.

His lips left hers and he planted little kisses on her cheeks, moving up to her eyes and then back down to her nose. That made her giggle.

He leaned back and smiled at her. "Liked that, did you?"

She sighed happily. "I can't believe this is happening. I keep wondering if it's all a dream and I'll wake up."

Lee stopped smiling. "Patience Primrose, I don't ever want you to talk like that again. You are such a beautiful and special person, it is I who feels lucky to have you!"

Her eyes teared up again. "Thank you for that, Lee."

He shook his head. "I'm going to make you a promise right here and now. I promise that I will do everything in my power to make sure that you never feel unworthy or unloved again. When you're feeling down, I'll be there. When you need someone to talk to, I'll be there.

"But you need to remember this, too. God will be there for both of us. If we pray together and always keep Him first in our lives, Patience, our lives will be so good together."

"I know," she told him in a shaky voice. "He's already done so much for me. He's given me two good friends and let me have that job when I really needed something for myself. But most of all, He's answered my prayer. I prayed that you'd be the one He chose for me, and He granted it!"

To Lee, it seemed like a good time for another kiss and he was just about to touch her lips with his own when the door to the doctor's office opened.

"Whoa there, boy! You haven't said your 'I do's' yet!" Caleb told them with a teasing glint in his eye as he came into the room.

Caleb wasn't the only one who entered. In walked Prudence and Mr. Touchet, also.

Protectively, Lee put his arm around Patience. He could feel her shaking, and he tightened his hold to reassure her.

"Patience, I'd like to talk to you. . . ," Mr. Touchet began.

"No!" Prudence interrupted. She stepped past him to get closer to Patience. "I want to tell her what I should have told her a long time ago."

She closed her eyes for a moment, then opened them. Her face was set with determination. "Twenty-two years ago, I got involved with Bernard. We courted for a short time, and I thought I loved him. He started pressuring me into having. . .relations. . .with him without the benefit of marriage. It was wrong and very much a sin, but I went along with it, thinking he would marry me."

Tears started filling her eyes, but she blinked them back and continued, "I became pregnant and I told him about it, hoping that we could hurry up and marry and nobody would find out. Well. . .he said he couldn't marry me because his family would never accept me. Instead he married someone else.

"My parents were horrified, and they did the first thing they thought of, and that was to send me off to Aunt Ida's house here in Springton. When I got here, it was Ida who thought up the idea of me being a widow. I went along with it and tried so hard to mold myself into a better person."

"You became a strict, religious-minded woman who wouldn't bend even for her own daughter," Patience spoke out, her voice scratchy from crying.

Prudence threw up her hands. "Don't you understand I didn't want you to end up like me? I did what I thought was best."

Patience stepped out from Lee's embrace and walked closer to her mother. "Couldn't you have just shown me a little attention? Couldn't you have loved me?" she cried out, pointing to her chest.

Prudence put a hand over her mouth as a sob rose out of her throat. "Oh, Patience. I do. . .love you. Please. . . please forgive me. Please. . ." She broke down completely and covered her face with both of her hands.

Huge tears rolled down Patience's cheeks. "Oh, Mama. . ." She wept and threw her arms around her mother. "I do. I do forgive you. I just never. . .knew. I never knew. . .you loved me."

Lee looked at the preacher and they shared an understanding glance. Caleb had apparently known about all this, because he didn't look surprised. Lee sure wished he'd known so he could have been prepared to say something to Patience to comfort her.

When they'd cried all their tears, the women separated, wiping their tear-stained faces.

Lee stepped forward and placed a hand on Patience's back. "Are you all right, darlin'?" he asked.

She nodded. "I'm okay."

He wasn't convinced, but they could talk about it later. He looked around the room and noticed that although the preacher was still with them, Mr. Touchet had slipped out of the room.

"He said that Patience needed to deal with one parent at a time. She can go and talk to him when she's ready," Brother Caleb told him.

Lee turned to Patience. "I think that is a good idea, don't you?"

She nodded wearily. "Yes, I'm a little overwhelmed, and I need time to think about it all."

He grimaced. "Well, this is probably not the best of circumstances to announce this, but Patience has agreed to marry me."

Prudence opened her mouth to say something, but Lee stopped her. "But not today!" he told her emphatically. "Patience should have a big wedding with a pretty dress and the whole works. She deserves it. But she also needs time to deal with her father being alive and the issues between you and she."

Prudence simply closed her mouth and nodded.

"In the meantime," the preacher spoke up, "why don't

all of you come over to the house? Rachel always cooks so much for the children, there's always plenty left. She'll want to hear the news of your engagement."

Lee threw Patience a questioning glance, and she nodded her head. He smoothed his hand up and down her back in a comforting gesture as they followed the preacher out of the office.

nineteen

On Christmas Eve morning, Patience was still in bed, though it was well past nine, dreaming of Lee.

It was such a beautiful dream. Lee was in his best suit, standing in a mist of clouds, reaching his hand out to her. He was smiling and telling her to. . . Hmmm. Patience couldn't quite make out what he was trying to tell her.

Patience tried to run closer, but as dreams sometimes went, her legs felt heavy and she was unable to get to him as fast as she wanted. Finally, she could hear him better. He was saying. . .

"Wake up, Patience!"

Wake up? That was a strange thing for him to say!

"Patience Anne, are you going to sleep all day?"

Patience was jolted awake by her mother's voice; Lee's voice drifted off into dreamland. Sleepily, she blinked and saw not only her mother but Susannah and Rachel standing by her bed.

"What are y'all doing here?"

Susannah giggled in her delightful way, and Rachel put her hands on her hips and shook her head. "Patience, as much as you longed for this day to come, I can't believe you have to ask that! We're here to help you get ready!" Rachel explained.

Patience sat up then. Suddenly, her heart filled with gladness and her stomach fluttered with excitement. Of course! How could she have forgotten?

It was her wedding day!

Susannah ran to the window and pulled back the gingham curtain. "And look, Patience! It snowed last night! Just enough to make everything pretty and white!"

Patience crawled out of bed and looked at the snow-covered landscape. The sun was glistening through the iced-over trees, making them sparkle like jewels. It was all just perfect.

"It never snows at this time of the year," she commented.

"Well, Caleb would say that God likes to give wedding presents, too," Rachel said as she joined the women at the window.

Patience stared out and tried to blink back the tears that came to her eyes. "God has already done so much for me. I feel like I don't deserve any more!"

"Now, I won't hear talk like that, young lady!" her mother said from behind her in a brisk voice. Prudence's hands came to rest on Patience's shoulders, and she felt a warm feeling of contentment run through her that she was sure she'd never get used to. "You deserve all God has for you!"

Patience and her mother had come a long way since that confrontation in the jail two months earlier. With the pastor's help, they were able to work through their feelings and past fears and come to a closer relationship. They still had a ways to go, but God was surely working a miracle.

"Okay, enough dillydallying! We've got work to do!" Susannah said, stepping away from the window.

"We sure do," Rachel chimed in. "Your mother has fixed you a good breakfast, so you can get in there and eat. But you need to hurry, because we've got to do your hair. . ."

". . .And get that dress and veil on! With all those buttons, it's going to take awhile!" Susannah finished for her.

Patience laughed with delight. "Okay, okay! Boy, you two are bossy!" she exclaimed as she grabbed her robe and followed them into the dining room.

❧

After breakfast, they all went to Rachel's house so that they would be near the church. The three women worked for over an hour brushing, teasing, pinning, buttoning, and tugging. Patience stood or sat patiently as they did their jobs, wishing they would hand her a mirror so she could see the progress.

But as usual, Rachel liked to wait until everything was finished so she could make a grand production of it.

And *finally* she was ready. Patience stood in front of Rachel's oval floor mirror and stared at herself with awe and disbelief.

Her dress was made of the finest silk that Adelaide Hayes was able to buy. It was her gift to Patience. Rachel and Susannah had worked together on her dress and they'd done a superb job.

The gown was high at the neck and the bodice fashioned of the most delicate lace. The bell-like sleeves were puffy and fell inches above the elbow with an undersleeve fitted all the way to her wrist. The skirt was full, but smooth, gathered at the back and fastened by a large pearl-edged bow. The dress fit her figure perfectly.

Her hair was loosely knotted at her nape and parted down the middle, tendrils of blond curls framing her face. She wore a circlet of roses with a long lace veil attached to the back like a crown around her head.

Patience felt like a fairy princess.

Prudence walked up to stand beside her. There were tears in her eyes as she looked at her only daughter through the mirror. "I'm so proud of you, Patience. You really make a beautiful bride."

Patience smiled radiantly at her mother and hugged her. "Thank you, Mama," she whispered, squeezing her tightly.

After a moment, Susannah announced that it was time for them to go. She was in a pretty gown of green and was to be Patience's maid of honor.

A flutter of nervousness ran through Patience's stomach as she followed the women to the church. She felt a little like she was still walking around in her dream from this morning. It seemed to take forever to reach the church, although it was only a few steps away.

Bernard Touchet was waiting for her at the door. The dapper man that she had, just yesterday, agreed to call "Daddy" was to walk her down the aisle to her future husband.

Theirs was a relationship far from resolved, but they had made a few small steps on understanding what had happened years ago.

He'd explained to Patience and Prudence that he'd been pressured by his parents to marry someone else. And when Prudence had told him she was pregnant, he'd gotten scared and married the other girl. Because his wife was from South Louisiana, where his parents were originally from, he'd gone down there to live. He knew that he was running away from Prudence and their child, and he had never forgiven himself nor forgotten what he'd done.

He'd started his own rice farm, and he and his wife had planned to raise their children in the large plantation house that he built for them. But when his wife and his child died in childbirth, Bernard began to look for Prudence and Patience.

Unfortunately, her parents would not tell him where she was, and no one else in the town of Shreveport knew.

Off and on, he'd taken time off from his work to look for Prudence. His break came when he read in the paper about the Jenkins gang being arrested in Springton, Texas. It had told the details, commenting that Prudence Primrose had been kidnapped and then released by them.

Bernard had sold his farm and come to Springton in hopes of apologizing to Prudence. He knew it would not be easy for her to forgive him, but he hoped for some sort of place in both her and his daughter's life.

Prudence was still standoffish with him, but Patience knew that deep inside her mother still loved him and would soon be able to forgive him. Despite all that had happened, Patience couldn't help but want him in her life.

She'd so yearned for a father and now she had one. Life was too short to stay mad at one man and one woman's mistake.

That was the reason she asked her father to walk her down the aisle.

From inside the building, Patience could hear the strains of the wedding march beginning. Her mother kissed her on the cheek and allowed Jessie Stone, the pastor's son, to walk her into the church and show her to her seat.

Next, after throwing Patience a reassuring wink, Susannah walked in.

Rachel took the bride's hand and squeezed it. "Now it's your turn, Patience. Don't be nervous. You look beautiful," she told her with confidence.

Patience nodded her head and took a deep breath. "I'm ready," she told her father as she took his arm.

Slowly, they entered the church and began to walk down the aisle. She was so glad that the town had never found out about the incident at the jail. And where her father was concerned, they all assumed that he'd been thought dead from the war and they had been unable to find him. Patience and her mother did nothing to deny nor confirm the rumor. They all felt safer letting the townspeople think that than to allow her mother to feel more shame. And if anyone was a little confused about their last names being different, they were much too afraid of Prudence to ask.

Patience looked forward, to the front of the church. The preacher was standing there in the center, and then her eyes fell to the handsome man standing beside him.

Lee was dressed just like in her dream. So tall and handsome robed in his dark suit. He was staring at her with such a look of love that it nearly took her breath clean away.

She wanted to laugh when Billy, his best man, nudged him with his elbow and, when Lee glanced at him, wiggled his eyebrows and nodded in Patience's direction.

Lee just looked back at Patience and smiled proudly.

She was the luckiest woman in the world!

❧

Lee felt as though he was the luckiest man in the world. What a woman she was! And she was *his!*

His heart was pounding hard in his chest as his eyes

swept over his bride. She looked so beautiful in her white gown. The only color was the red Christmas flower in her hands.

It seemed fitting that they marry on such a holy day of celebration. Every year, from this day on, they would not only celebrate Christ's birth, but they would rejoice in their marriage as well.

Finally, she was beside him. Bernard guided her hand to Lee's arm, and Lee felt her sweetness and warmth as she held onto him.

He didn't think. He just bent down and placed a gentle kiss on her smooth cheek.

A tinkle of laughter drifted over the congregation, and Caleb gave them a mock frown. "You're supposed to wait until the end of the service for that!"

Lee felt his face burn, and he smiled sheepishly at Caleb. "Sorry," he whispered. He glanced at Patience and relaxed when he saw her trying to hold back a laugh.

The ceremony was beautiful. There wasn't a dry eye in the whole place by the time it was through. And when Lee finally got another chance to kiss his bride, every female heart went to fluttering as they dreamed of their own weddings past and future.

epilogue

After a two-week trip to New Orleans, a wedding present from Bernard Touchet, Patience and Lee returned to Springton. So many things had happened, they soon realized, while they were honeymooning.

First, the Powell brothers—the outlaws that had shot Patience—had been arrested in Oklahoma and it looked like there weren't going to be any jailbreaks this time.

Second, they found out that Patience's mama and daddy had gotten married in a quiet ceremony at the pastor's house. According to Prudence, it was so that they could live in the same house together to stifle any gossip. But Patience saw the emotions that passed between her parents and knew that it was a happy union.

Third, Lee had a friend in the Rangers who was part of the crowd that welcomed him and Patience home. And he'd told them that he'd been down in South Texas for the last few weeks and reported that El Paso was "so cold that icicles were hanging from the cactus." Somehow, that *didn't* surprise the happy couple.

But once everybody left them at the train station, they headed out to her mother's old farm and began to move her things into his house.

She was busy hanging her dresses in his wardrobe and he was unpacking a box of books. "Remind me to give Bobby Joe his books back. He let me borrow a few of his, and I've forgotten all about returning them," she said as she shook the wrinkles out of one of her best dresses.

"Well, darlin', I would hope that Bobby Joe wasn't in your thoughts while we were honeymooning!"

She rolled her eyes at his mock jealousy.

They worked quietly for a few moments until Lee began to chuckle. "I don't think this one belongs to Bobby Joe!"

She looked over her shoulder to see what he was talking about and froze.

In his hand was Emma Hadley's book, *A Young Lady's Guide to Courtship and Marriage!*

She dropped the dress and ran over to take the book. "Give me that!"

He held it high and shook his head. "Wait! I want to see what this says!" He opened up the book, still holding it over his head and out of her reach. " 'Batting your eyelashes and giving a gentle giggle lets a gentleman know that you have his complete interest. A gentleman always likes to feel as though he is the most important man in the room,' " Lee read aloud.

He looked at her with disbelief. "That's why you were batting your lashes? Because you read it in a book?"

She had never been so embarrassed in her life! She could have sworn she threw that book away a long time ago! "Oh, give me that! And quit laughing!"

"I thought you had something wrong with your eyes!" Lee exclaimed and began to chuckle.

She finally was able to grab the book out of his hand. She whirled around, intent on leaving the room, when he grabbed her arm.

"Ah, don't leave, sweetheart! I was just joking!" He lifted her chin so she would look at him. He shrugged his shoulders. "Hey, it worked, didn't it?" he said arrogantly.

She rolled her eyes and hit him playfully with the book. "Oh, please! Is that your head I see swelling?"

He laughed and with a flick of his wrist tugged the book away from her and tossed it across the room so that he could take her into his arms. Holding her close, he put his face near to hers so that their foreheads touched.

"Why didn't I realize that you were the one for me right away? Then you wouldn't have had to read that book and follow that awful advice!"

She sighed. "Because you thought Susannah was the perfect one for you."

"Nah. . .I think that I was just fighting my feelings for you and using her as a shield. But know this, darlin', I thank God that He opened my eyes, and I'll never let you go!"

"That's good, because I wasn't planning on letting you go!" she said saucily, then gave him a kiss that made his head spin.

A Letter To Our Readers

Dear Reader:

In order that we might better contribute to your reading enjoyment, we would appreciate your taking a few minutes to respond to the following questions. We welcome your comments and read each form and letter we receive. When completed, please return to the following:

Rebecca Germany, Fiction Editor
Heartsong Presents
PO Box 719
Uhrichsville, Ohio 44683

1. Did you enjoy reading *Courtin' Patience?*
   ❑ Very much. I would like to see more books by this author!
   ❑ Moderately
   I would have enjoyed it more if ______________

   ____

   ____

2. Are you a member of **Heartsong Presents**? Yes ❑ No ❑
   If no, where did you purchase this book? ____________

   ____

3. How would you rate, on a scale from 1 (poor) to 5 (superior), the cover design? ____________________________

4. On a scale from 1 (poor) to 10 (superior), please rate the following elements.

   _____ Heroine _____ Plot

   _____ Hero _____ Inspirational theme

   _____ Setting _____ Secondary characters

5. These characters were special because________________

____

____

6. How has this book inspired your life?________________

____

____

7. What settings would you like to see covered in future **Heartsong Presents** books?________________

____

____

8. What are some inspirational themes you would like to see treated in future books?________________

____

____

9. Would you be interested in reading other **Heartsong Presents** titles? Yes ❑ No ❑

10. Please check your age range:

❑ Under 18	❑ 18-24	❑ 25-34
❑ 35-45	❑ 46-55	❑ Over 55

11. How many hours per week do you read?________________

Name ____________________________________

Occupation ________________________________

Address __________________________________

City ____________ State ________ Zip ________

Relax this Christmas

And enjoy the Christmas Season with our two new novella collections–*Fireside Christmas* and *Winter Wishes*–both have four new stories in one big volume for only $7.94 for the pair.

Experience love stories from days gone by in ***Fireside Christmas*** as Kristin Billerbeck, Peggy Darty, Rosey Dow, and JoAnn A. Grote take you back to simpler times.

Brand-new stories from today abound with love and charm in ***Winter Wishes*** when you curl up with Yvonne Lehman, Loree Lough, Colleen L. Reece, and Debra White Smith as they tell you about modern day romances.

♥ ♥ ♥ ♥ ♥ ♥ ♥ ♥ ♥ ♥ ♥ ♥ ♥ ♥ ♥ ♥ ♥

Please send me ____ copies of *Fireside Christmas* and ____ copies of *Winter Wishes*. I am enclosing $4.97 each. Or send me ____ set(s) for $7.94.

(Please add $1.00 to cover postage and handling per order. OH add 6% tax.)

Send check or money order, no cash or C.O.D.s please.

Name ________________________________

Address ________________________________

City, State, Zip ________________________________

To place a credit card order, call 1-800-847-8270.

Send to: Heartsong Presents Reader Service, PO Box 719, Uhrichsville, OH 44683

♥ ♥ ♥ ♥ ♥ ♥ ♥ ♥ ♥ ♥ ♥ ♥ ♥ ♥ ♥ ♥ ♥